TV Develo

How an *Idea* becomes a TV Show

First Updated Edition

MW01492225

By Stephanie Varella

DEDICATION

To my sweet, inspiring,
beautiful and wise daughter,
Sage.

TABLE OF CONTENTS

Table Of Contents

Table Of Contents

Words with single quotes denote TV industry terms, which are defined in the Glossary.

ACKNOWLEDGMENTS

A SINCERE THANK YOU TO:

Susan Musillo for all her help with this book. She inspired me to write it, edited it and encouraged me throughout the process.

Lew Musillo for his steadfast support and all he did to advance the completion of this book.

The industry professionals who generously contributed and shared their experiences.

My students, the next generation of TV developers, who inspire me every day.

TEASER

Do you think your life would make a great TV show?

Almost every person, after I've told them that I develop TV shows for a living, tells me about an idea, or that their life would make a great show. The truth is creating a TV series is not as easy as one might think.

In the 1990s, when I started working in the entertainment business, there were certain do's and don'ts about how to develop TV shows. Today, however, A LOT has changed. Back then there were just a few networks you could pitch to in order to sell your show. There were "rules" about what you could and could not develop. For example, shows had to have a specific structure to them. They had to have characters who were likable and non-offensive. Overnight ratings were everything! Today the measure of success is so much more. It's all about getting a second season, critical acclaim, awards, cutting through the clutter, ratings and getting subscribers!

Also, since TV had been around for many decades, it was difficult to come up with an original idea because it seemed that everything had already been done. On top of that, this was a huge challenge because the shows had to appeal to a mass audience. That is not at all the case today.

At the time, I was a young, eager, green (newbie) executive. All I knew was that I loved watching TV. I was the kid who couldn't get enough of it. In college, we had parties centered around watching TV shows. It was a fun to get together each week to find out what was going to happen with our favorite shows.

When I moved to Los Angeles from New York in 1993, one week after I graduated from college, I knew one thing. I wanted to work in entertainment. I had no idea what anyone did, other than the actors… and I knew I didn't want to be an actor. I bought a one-way ticket, knew absolutely no one, sent my boxes to an address sight unseen and started my new life. Somehow, I knew I was meant to live in LA. It may not be for everyone, but for me I loved the weather... and it felt so clean, so open, and so full of possibilities.

My first job was at a very big and famous talent agency, The William Morris Agency (WMA). Prior to this, I had several internships where I worked in casting and as a production assistant. But this was my first real, paying job and it was a great foray into the business. Initially I thought I wanted to learn about making movies (feature films), because I loved movies. However, the only desk that was available at that time was in 'TV Talent.' Of course, I took it. Getting this first TV job opened my eyes to a business that I had not considered at all up to this point and yet would find myself enjoying, thriving and spending the rest of my career pursuing.

It didn't take long for me to find out that TV Talent is the department that works with actors and fills all the acting jobs on TV. At that time the big stars didn't want to act on TV shows…they wanted to be on the "big screen" vs. the "small screen." They believed that TV was sort of a step down for them. Also, the independent ('Indie') movies were for up and coming actors, not big stars. But, over the course of my career, I have seen all of that change.

When I think back about that first position at WMA, the only way I am able to describe it is that it was like being in a sorority or fraternity. The other assistants were my pledge brothers and sisters. We worked from 8:30 a.m. to 11:30 p.m. every day and on weekends. It was a whirlwind of hard work, but we gained tons of knowledge and experience in a relatively short period of time. We were exhausted, but we loved it. To this day I am friends with many of those assistants. Some of them became top executives of their field. Some stayed in the agency/management world, some became development executives at networks and studios, and a few became producers and/or writers. Overall, I found it to be a fulfilling experience and very beneficial for networking in the business.

After a year, I was ready to leave WMA because I knew I did not want to become an agent. The first non-agency job I heard about was in TV Development. Since I had worked in 'TV Talent,' I didn't know what it was development people did, but I was eager to find out.

In the mid 1990s, I was lucky to be offered an assistant position at Spelling Entertainment. I remember AARON SPELLING (from whom I learned so much) used to say that "Stars make movies. Television makes stars." So true! He was a legend in the TV business. He was a producer who re-invented TV shows every decade for 40-50 years. It isn't likely there will be another like him, probably not in my lifetime.

While at Spelling Entertainment, I went from being an assistant to a young development executive. It was there that I learned all about what TV development is, and now I am able to pass on that knowledge to you with this book. My mentor was JENNIFER NICHOLSON. During the six years I was there she taught me how TV shows were developed. She got married, became JENNIFER SALKE and had three babies during that time. She went on to become the head of 20th Century FOX Studios, the number two executive at NBC, and is now the head of Amazon Studios. She is one of the top female executives in the TV business today.

While working at Spelling Entertainment, I was very proud of the fact I was part of the team that helped AARON SPELLING become the record holder of the most scripted shows on TV at one time, which was nine.*

> *Side note: *Months before going to print on this book, this record was broken by a writer/producer - GREG BERLANTI. He has fourteen shows in production (9/2018). It is important to remember that today there are over 50 places to sell to. When*

AARON SPELLING was producing, there were only six. Having nine shows at six places is an amazing feat, and it took 18 years for someone to break that record!

When I started working as Vice President of Series Development and Production for JERRY BRUCKHEIMER in September of 2001, although he was very successful film producer, most people did not know who he was. Once **CSI** became a huge hit that next year, he became a household name. It was incredible to be there at that exact moment in time. **CSI: Las Vegas** and **Amazing Race** were just about to premiere and, during my tenure there, we grew to having seven shows (scripted and unscripted) on the air at one time! This is still his personal best.

Today, there are more TV shows in production than ever before and over 50 outlets to sell shows. Everything I learned and saw back when I started has literally been turned on its head. There are no more rules, meaning you can pretty much develop any kind of show you want and you will probably find a home for it.

It's the Golden Age of the TV business and it's also the Wild Wild West!

*****

To The Reader:

My hope in writing this book is that people who are thinking about getting into the TV business will now have a foundation and better understanding from which to build their journey.

One of the things I've done in the past few years is to create and teach a course on TV Development at UCLA Extension, and to offer private consultations through TVDevelopmentcoach.com. To my surprise, I discovered that there were no other classes like it, and there is no book on the market today that explains how an idea becomes a TV show before it is produced. So here it is.

Many people wouldn't think there is a specific process when developing a TV show and as a development executive, you normally do not get a "credit" on the show, but there is a team of people who truly contribute to the show beyond the credits.

I hope you can see from this publication how much I enjoy developing TV shows. Being a part of a business that impacts people personally, and both influences and reflects world affairs, has always been fascinating and thrilling to me. I hope your journey brings you as much satisfaction.

I am really proud of the projects I have personally been a part of developing, whether they ended up getting on the air or not. When they are successful, wow! It's awesome. There is truly nothing like it.

So whether you want to write, direct, produce for television, or have a more secure position as a development executive, this book is a great way to start.

With respect and gratitude,
Stephanie

WHAT YOU CAN LEARN FROM THIS BOOK

- How to transform an idea into a TV series

- To think about TV in a more comprehensive and expansive way

- What TV Development is and how it works

- What is and isn't working on the TV landscape

- How to move forward with your own project

- How to build a career in TV Development

- The dynamics between the writer and the producer

- What goes into selling a TV show

- What studios and networks are looking for in a TV series

- Who the players are in TV Development

- Where ideas come from for TV projects

- A good idea vs. a not-so-good idea for a TV show

- Whether or not you should pursue a particular project

- How to copyright your idea

- The different formats of episodic television

- The tools to protect ideas and get options on intellectual properties (IPs)

- How to pitch your project

WHAT YOU CAN LEARN FROM THIS BOOK

- The best ways to present your project

- The pitching process for the networks

- What's included in a pitch document

- A good pitch vs. a not-so-good pitch

- How to improve the quality of your pitch

- How to get a pitch meeting with the network

- The standard, older ways of pitching vs. the new ways

- What a sizzle reel is?

- Why you should or shouldn't produce a sizzle reel

- The process of developing original scripts with a studio and network

- What a bible is for a TV series and how to put one together

- How a script is developed with a writer and a producer

- The importance of a script when developing a TV show

- How notes fit into the development process

- The best approach to give notes to a writer

- What a writers list is and how to put one together

- Where to sell your idea(s)

- Understanding the marketplace, the buyers and the outlets

- The current networks/buyers

WHAT YOU CAN LEARN FROM THIS BOOK

- Which network to pitch to and when

- How to define your audience for each project

- How to identify the different audiences at the various outlets

- Where and how to sell your show

- The differences in selling to a broadcast network vs. a streaming or premium outlet

- Projections for the future of TV

- The relationship between studios and their partnerships with networks/buyers

- How acquisitions work

- The different types of deals and packages in television

- How to get attachments

- How to market your project

- The importance of a competitive development report

- How to develop a strategy for your project

- What a transmedia campaign is and how it is useful

- What agents, managers and development executives (studio and network) say about developing TV shows

- How the TV business has dramatically changed in the last two decades

- The steps to take after reading this book

ACT ONE

What is 'TV Development'?

When I went to college, there were no classes to take on Television Development. There were media classes, writing classes and acting classes, but there was nothing about how TV shows were developed and got on the air. Even today, this is not something that is offered in most schools. As I mentioned (in the teaser), I am teaching a course, at UCLA Extension, the first of its kind (that I know of).

When I fell into working in TV Development in the mid-1990s, little did I know it would be something I would be doing for the next 20+ years. One thing I learned was that it can be a very lucrative career of choice. Although there is a paucity of current salary information for TV executives out there today, I hope the following gives you some idea of what you can earn.

In 2017, one of the highest paid network executives (who was recently ousted) CBS's LES MOONVES, made a whopping $69.3 million! (*The Observer*, 2018, *by Sissi Cao*)

Another top TV executive Steve Mosko, earned $2.8 million (plus bonuses) in 2015 as SONY's president. (*Hollywood Reporter*, "Hollywood Salaries Revealed" 2015, by Austin Siegemund-Broka and Paul Bond)

Here are some statistics from 2012. (*Vulture Magazine*, "Polone: So How Much Do Hollywood Players Make?" 2012, by Gavin Polone) Gavin Polone is a very successful agent turned producer.

STUDIO

- A major TV Chairman/President/CEO gets $2 million-$5 million per year.

- The Executive Vice President (the person running both comedy and drama development) makes $600,000 - $1 million per year.

- The Vice President (there is usually one for comedy and one for drama) gets $250,000 - $500,000 per year.

- The Director level executive makes $100,000 - $250,000 per year.

NETWORK

- The Entertainment President makes $2.5 million-$5 million per year.

- The Executive Vice President (the person running both comedy and drama development) makes $750,000 - $1.5 million per year.

- The Vice President (comedy or drama development) makes $250,000-$500,000 per year.

- The Director level executive makes $125,000-$200,000 per year.

Like most kids, I loved watching TV when I was growing up. Of course my mom, like most parents, objected to too much TV. But I am here to report that those hours spent in front of the TV have paid off because it gave me the foundation of knowledge about TV shows. Even today, with my own young child, I see that most of her friends' parents would like to keep their children's TV watching at a minimum. There has been study after study telling us that watching a lot of TV is bad for us. I am neither a doctor, nor an expert on the science of human interaction with electronics, but I believe, like everything in life, *moderation* is the key.

There is, indeed, a lot of excellent content on many of the networks today. I believe this is where it all must begin. For anyone to work in television development, whether you are a writer, producer, actor, director, or executive, one must have *passion* and love for the art of television shows.

> New FOX CEO of Entertainment (former AMC President) CHARLIE COLLIER said, "I think anyone who gets into the business and who doesn't have a healthy appreciation for the content and the brilliant people who create the best of it, is in the wrong business." *("The Future of Television" by Pamela Douglas p.56)*

I couldn't agree more. Today, with more shows than ever, watching all of them is impossible. But when you watch one that speaks to you, it can't get any better than that.

In order to understand what TV Development is, we need to know a little about the history of the television.

HISTORY OF THE TELEVISION IN A NUTSHELL

"Television" literally means long-distance sight or far vision by wireless transmission. When it was first invented, far vision meant across a room. Later it meant across a country, and now it's around the world.

Similar to other amazing inventions and historical truths, several people around the globe were inventing this life-changing device, later known as, the television, at the same time.

Approximately 5,000-6,000 years ago, people began recording history. They were literally writing words down for the first time to record what was going on at the time. The amazing thing was that this didn't just happen in one place in the world. It happened simultaneously in different places around the world, and these first historians had no idea about each other. This interesting phenomenon occurred with the invention of television as well.

WHO INVENTED THE TELEVISION?

That depends on who you ask. Giving credit to the first person who invented something has become easier over time because of the advancement of technology. But, back when TV was being invented, it happened in bits and pieces. One person invented a part of it, and then another took it a step further, and so on. That is the reason why the inventor of the TV is a hotly disputed subject.

Here are the three people around the globe who are credited with invention of the television:

An American - PHILO FARNSWORTH
A Russian - VLADIMIR KOSMA ZWORYKIN
A Brit - JOHN BAIRD

Each contributed to its advancement, and suffice it to say we are very thankful to these inventors and the people who helped them because we are so fortunate to have the wonderful gift of TELEVISION.

One of the most important progressions for television was in the 1950s when color TV was introduced by CBS and RCA Victor. The initial RCA Victor color TV set cost $1,000 in 1954 and was in four out of ten homes. Today's equivalent would be about $6,500. It wasn't perfect, but people loved it. Gathering around the TV became mainstream around the world.

At the same time, TV viewers were introduced to a little device called, "lazy bones," which was invented by the Zenith Corporation. This is better known as the remote control. It should be noted that inventors had developed remote-controlled electronics before this, but it wasn't until the 1950s that the remote control was invented for television. At first, they were connected by a bulky wire.   Then in 1955, Eugene Polley invented the "Flashmatic," which was the first wireless remote. Today voice control is available on some systems and I believe will soon be commonplace.

TV took another huge step forward in the late nineties when a device called, TIVO, was introduced.   For me this was a game changer. I could finally pause a show, go to another show, watch it and come back to the original one I was watching. I was also able to record shows and watch them whenever I wanted. Probably the biggest concern the TV industry had about this device was the fact that the viewer didn't need to watch commercials anymore.

I was working in the industry at that time, and I remember we were all wondering how the advertisers were going to get passed this.   Here it is, twenty years later, and while advertisers have been finding new ways to get the word out about their products, commercials are still being aired on TV shows and the viewers are still fast-forwarding over them.

Today, we have more channels and options than ever before; where you watch (TVs are everywhere), what you watch, how you watch (live or recorded), on which device, on which network, etc. One can only wonder where or what is next for the evolution of television.

Television Development

Let's take a look at the various roles people have in TV Development.

THE PLAYERS:

WRITERS

EXECUTIVE PRODUCERS

PRODUCERS

STUDIO EXECUTIVES

NETWORK EXECUTIVES

BUSINESS AFFAIRS EXECUTIVES

WRITERS

This is where is all begins. Writers are the ones who literally create, dream, envision, and tell the stories that ultimately sell and become TV shows. It is their vision that an executive producer (if attached) must be as equally passionate about and support.

The writer/creator is most often attached as an executive producer. She or he is called, the "creator," and would get "created by" credit on the show. If it's their first project, sometimes they will start with a co-executive producer (Co-EP) credit before being elevated to executive producer, but they would always get the "created by" credit. This is mandated by the Writer's Guild of America (WGA).

Act 1

EXECUTIVE PRODUCERS

An Executive Producer (EP) is a creative partner to a writer. They help facilitate the writer's vision by assisting in setting up the project either at a studio and/or network or through independent financing. They can be either writing or non-writing executive producers. The writing executive producers are known as 'showrunners.' Writers can bring an idea to an EP, or the EP can bring one to them. Together they shape the idea into a series and bring it to life.

A non-writing EP always needs a writer/creator. In order to sell and produce a series with a network/buyer, they need to know the writer's vision. There is a particular circumstance where an EP can bring an IP (*more on "IPs" in Act 2*), or an idea, to a network without a writer and enlist their help to find the writer, but networks would not buy the idea until the writer is attached.

PRODUCERS

In the credits of a TV show you will see many names with different types of "producer" credits. These are the writers and/or physical producers on the show. The writers work in the writer's room with the creator of the series and help 'break the story' for each episode in the season(s). Oftentimes they will write episodes of the series. The 'below the line,' or physical producers, on the show help with the actual production of the show.

STUDIO EXECUTIVES

The Studio Executive is the person who works for the company that 'deficit finances' the project. The studio owns the show. Deficit finance means the studio will pay the amount of money it costs to produce the show above and beyond what they get from the network.

Act 1

NETWORK EXECUTIVES

The Network Executive is the person who works for the company that pays a 'license fee' for the project in order to air it on their network. A license fee is an actual fee that the show (the studio) gets from the network for the right to air it. It's like renting vs. owning. The network, in turn, will charge advertisers a fee to place ads (commercials) during the show.

At the network and the studio, as well as some production companies (companies that writers and producers form), there can be two types of executives: Development and Current.

- Development Executives develop the pilot for the series.
- Current Executives work on the life of the series while it is on-the-air, in 'first run.' First run is the first airing of a show.

BUSINESS AFFAIRS EXECUTIVES

The Business Affairs Executive is an entertainment attorney who works for either the studio or the network. She or he makes all the deals. (*More on "Deals" in Act 3*)

THE PROCESS: HOW DO THEY ALL WORK TOGETHER?

Writer(s), with or without non-writing **producer(s)**, bring their ideas to **studio executives**…

They then work together on the "project" and bring it to the buyers, **the network executives**…

All of them work in concert on the project and, hopefully, it becomes a SERIES!

If you are wondering whether writers can sell their ideas directly to a network without a studio and/or have a non-writing producer attached, the answer is yes.

It is not necessary to have all these people and/or elements attached to projects to get it sold, but in my experience it is a rare show that is sold from a writer directly to a network.

When writers do 'pitch' directly to a network without a studio and/or producers attached, it would require the network executives to put more work into the project. This is in part because the studio and/or producers usually get a project to a certain level before bringing it to the network. When a project comes to a network with 'attachments' already in place, the network can and will probably have a better idea of what they are buying. On the flip side if the network gets involved in bringing on elements, they will have more of a say/control with the project and in turn, become more invested.

THE BIGGEST MISCONCEPTION ABOUT TV DEVELOPMENT:

I have found the biggest misconception people have is when they believe they have a great idea for a TV show, they also believe it should, and could be easily made into one. My hope with this book is that you will see there is much more than meets the eye when developing TV shows. Also, that every great idea does not translate into a viable TV show.

KIDS PROGRAMMING

When I was growing up, Saturday morning was dedicated to kids programming. Now there are entire networks that specifically develop and cater to kids (i.e., Disney Channel, Nickelodeon, Cartoon Network).

Kids programming is run a bit differently than 'prime time.' Prime time is programming for adults, ages 18-49, which is the most coveted demographic. Prime time is considered to be after dinner and before bedtime, or from 8:00–10:00 p.m.

How is kids programming different? One big difference is that the network and studio usually act as one entity. This business model has its advantages, they own the show and also because profits from the shows are made in more ways than just advertising. They have things like merchandising, which is a very important factor.

Additionally, kids programming usually doesn't have separate executives working on the pilots *and* the series. Sometimes they do have different departments for Current and Development, but most of the time they have executives that develop and also work on the shows on the air.

Another big difference is that kids programming also has movie and animation departments that complement their series development, although not all of them do.

When I first started to learn about kids programming, I was really surprised to hear that ideas are usually developed in-house or internally, which means the network executives generate or come up with ideas themselves. Then they pitch the idea (could even be just a title) to a writer(s), who comes back with a more detailed pitch on the idea. The network then decides which take they like the best. This is definitely not how shows are developed for other networks, but it is very similar to the way that feature (movie) film development works. However, it is still possible and definitely does occur where producers and/or writers bring in pitches and/or completed 'spec' scripts for consideration.

A 'spec' script is a pilot script that a writer writes before being commissioned, or paid, to write it. Writers write specs in order to display their writing skills and their "voice." It is a sample of their writing. (*More on this in Act 2*)

REALITY PROGRAMMING

When I started working in TV, there were not many reality shows. However, in the last twenty years there has been a sea change in the industry. Reality shows are quite prevalent and there are probably more of them than any other format in today's TV marketplace. (*More on "Formats" in Act 2*)

They can be game shows (*American Idol, The Voice*), docudramas (*Keeping up with the Kardashians, Housewives of...*) and everything in between (*Survivor, The Bachelor*, etc.). There are even several networks that produce only reality shows (HGTV, TLC, The Food Network, TruTV).

Probably the best time in history to sell a reality show is right now!

WHAT IS A REALITY TV SHOW?

A reality TV show is supposed to be a television show without a script, but most of them are actually semi-scripted and manipulated. This changes the authenticity of the show because the producers are providing made-up scenarios for the cast to engage in. This is different than scripted shows where the actors are acting and reciting lines from a script.

On reality shows, the participants are not acting, they are being themselves. The viewer watches and follows "real" people who purportedly speak their truths. For this reason, I believe the most important consideration in making a reality show is the casting. Finding the right people is critical. They must be inherently interesting and watchable.

The irony is that sometimes, especially if the acting is really good, a scripted show can seem more real, or authentic, than a reality show. This is due in part to the practice of manipulation on semi-scripted reality shows. In the history of television, the lines between reality and scripted are more blurred than ever before.

In the early 1990s, reality shows were becoming more popular because it was considered less expensive programming for prime-time. While at BRUCKHEIMER TV, I had the privilege of working on ABC's *Profiles from the Front Lines* and CBS's *The Amazing Race*. I experienced first-hand the development and production of these very ambitious and unique reality shows.

The Amazing Race was a very fun experience for me starting with the casting, where we met with many couples who were trying out for the show. They had to go through meetings, tests and even medical evaluations before being chosen.   It was an important process because we had to make sure they were physically and mentally fit to race.

It was truly a wild ride working as an executive on *Race*. I was in and out of each city literally within three days. I followed contestants as they ran the race with the camera and sound crews running with them. Much of the time the crews were running backwards! There was very little eating, sleeping and showering. No time for anything but the racing. Throughout the experience, I got to see what people are truly made of, which really came to life in the post-production of the show.

I worked on the first five seasons and it won an Emmy every year for "Outstanding Reality Competition Program."   If I could have chosen only one reality show to be on, it would have been *Race*… but working on it was the next best thing!

HOW TO DEVELOP A REALITY SHOW

If you are interested in developing a reality TV show, one of the first things you must figure out is what will be happening in each episode?   How will every season unfold?   If you put your thoughts and ideas down on paper, in detail in a 'treatment' form, you can protect it by registering it with the WGA. (*See Act 2 for details on protecting your work*)

The next step would be to research which production companies are already producing similar shows.   Then, call or email them.

They are always looking for new ideas, so it can't hurt to start with a phone call or email. Another way to present your idea is to shoot a sizzle/proof of concept reel. For a reality show, the sizzle reel is a shorter version, or part of an actual episode and can/ should include potential casting ideas. (*See "Sizzle Reels" in Act 2*)

THE "BUSINESS" OF THE TV BUSINESS

As you can imagine, the business side of television is all about the dollars and cents, which of course is extremely important. It is always about the bottom line, profits and what makes sense financially. However, I will not spend a lot of time covering this topic because, it is not my area of expertise. There are many books dedicated to the business side of television as well as people more qualified to discuss this, like the entertainment attorneys. But I will give you a basic understanding, which I believe is crucial for working in TV.

In the previous section entitled, "The Players: Network Executives," I explained how a network makes money from advertisers by charging them for commercials. This is one way networks make money. The way studios, either attached to a network (sometimes called, 'sister studio') or independent, make money is by owning and then selling produced and aired shows in syndication (re-runs) and internationally.

Studios can also become partners with another studio. As partners they deficit finance the show together. By doing so, they split in the rights to sell it domestically and internationally, then share in the profits. One reason independent studios will partner with network-owned (sister) studios is to have them (the network that bought the show) more invested, emotionally and financially, in the success of the series. That network will usually promote and stay with the show longer when their sister studio is attached to it. However, most studios would prefer to own the entire show and not partner on it because then they would make all of the profit. But, of course, that only happens when the show is successful. On the other hand, having a partner would be a good thing if the show fails because there is usually a significant amount of a financial loss. It's the old adage, "Less risk-less reward, high risk-high reward."

In 2016:

ABC owned or co-owned 9 out of 10 new series.
CBS owned or co-owned all 10 of its new scripted series.
FOX fully-owned 9 out of 10 new series.
NBC owned or co-owned all but three new series, 9 out of 12.

In 2017:

ABC owned or co-owned pilot 7 out of 12 new series.
CBS owned or co-owned 6 out of 8 new series.
FOX fully-owned 11 of their new series.
NBC fully-owned 11 of their new series.

One of the reasons this model poses a problem is because in essence it shuts out independents. In 1970, the FCC dealt with this issue.

WHAT IS THE FCC AND ITS IMPACT ON TV?

The Federal Communications Commission (FCC) is an independent agency of the United States government created to regulate interstate communications by radio, television, wire, satellite and cable. In 1970, it wanted to prevent the "Big Three" networks, ABC, CBS, and NBC, from monopolizing all broadcasting so it ruled that networks could not own any of the programming (shows) that aired in prime time (from 8:00-10:00 p.m.). This was a VERY BIG DEAL. It completely altered the relationship between the networks and television producers, and created a huge opportunity for independent TV companies. Many shows, like *The Mary Tyler Moore Show* and *All in the Family,* were made possible because of this rule.

In the 1980s, these rules were relaxed because networks could not maximize their profits. In the 1990s, the rules were repealed. All this led us to where we are today with the networks owning most of what they air. This effectively shuts out independents, but with the rise of the streaming networks, the doors have opened yet again for new, independently produced shows.

Nowadays, anyone with a camera and a computer can put a show on the air (e.g., YouTube). However, the downside is that no one is getting the mass audiences they got when there were only three channels... and probably never will again.

WHAT'S THE DIFFERENCE BETWEEN DEVELOPING A TV SERIES VS. A MOVIE?

It is important to understand that not every idea can be both. In fact, most ideas lend themselves to be either a TV show or a movie, usually not both. There are plenty of examples where TV shows became movies and vice versa, but in general here's what to look for in TV shows vs. movies:

TV SHOWS

TV shows are about relationships. They are intimate and have stories viewers can relate to. Whether watching them alone or with others, and often at home, these are stories that connect to contemporary experiences and issues that matter. Viewers become invested in the characters and want to watch them either week after week or 'binge watch.' Stories can have either a longer arc ('serialized'), which is told over time/season(s), or they can be franchised, which are episodic and told in one hour or less.

MOVIES

In general, movies are about a specific incident(s) or event that shaped/changed a person's life significantly. There is a very distinct beginning, middle and end that can be told in about two hours. The audience must feel some satisfaction at the end of the movie.

HYBRID

An example of a hybrid TV series and feature film is a 'miniseries.' Miniseries have the same elements of a movie, but because they have more story or content that fits into a two-hour format, they fall into the miniseries category. *(More on Formats in Act 2)*

*****

Questions To Consider

- Are you more of an "ideas" person or a writer?

- If you aspire to be a writer, how much have you written?

- What do you watch? What kinds of shows are they?

- What are your feelings about the shows that are on TV today?

- What kinds of TV shows/genres/do you feel are missing on the today's TV landscape today?

- If you were a network president, which network would you want to run and why? What would your mandate/'brand' be and why?

*****

ACT TWO

The Development Process

THE IDEA

If you want to develop a TV show, you have to start with a "great" idea or concept. "Great" being the operative word because what you or I think is a great may indeed be great, but there are other considerations that also have to be met.

Good timing is imperative. Your idea has to be what a network executive is looking for at that moment in time. For an idea to develop into a show, a group of people (writers, producers, and network executives) at a specific moment in time have what they believe is a great idea for a show. Together, and with you, they work on it, develop it, and then work on it some more. In the end, they do everything they possibly can for it to become a TV series.

Here's what some of the top TV executives have to say about ideas/concepts for TV shows:

> "There's no room for mediocrity" says, PATRICK MORAN, head of ABC. "It's the end of 'Who gives a shit?' television. It all has to be great." (_Vulture,_ _"The Business of Too Much TV,"_ _2016, by Josef Adalian and Maria Elena Fernandez_)

> Veteran showrunner CARLTON CUSE (_Lost,_ _Bates Motel_) said, "...so many networks and producers scramble again and again to make television that's great, finding standout ideas and then turning them into actual shows has perhaps never been more difficult." (_Vulture,_ _"The Business of Too Much TV," 2016, by Josef Adalian_ _and Maria Elena Fernandez_)

> Writer/Producer TREY CALLAWAY (_Revolu-_ _tion_) said, "One not entirely healthy change the TV business is borrowing from the feature business is that their source materials have become extremely important, in some cases too important. It's not enough to have a great original idea for a series. It's often as important to have source materials behind it - a book, comic book, previous television series, 'based on a...' It gives networks and studios a comfort level, feeling like they're plugging into an existing track record." (_"The Future of Television" by, Pamela_ _Douglas p.56)_

WHERE DO IDEAS COME FROM?

Ideas can and do come from anywhere, however...

When I started out as a young development executive, it was said that coming up with a new idea was nearly impossible. At that time, 50 years of television shows had already been produced, so how could anyone possibly come up with a new idea? I have learned that there are several ways to come up with new ideas.

Here are some, as follows:

1. ORIGINAL IDEAS

There will always will be original ideas. Meaning someone created the concept on their own and there is nothing else like it. It is totally unique. An idea can come from you, your friend, a family member, or anyone. It can be something that happened, or is happening, to you, or someone you know, or not, and it can be based in a totally fictitious place. It's an idea that is different than anything that has been produced or published. Some examples of this are *Orphan Black, Black Mirror, Six Feet Under,* and *X-Files.*

• A NEW VERSION OF AN OLD IDEA

Another way, which is not very novel, happens to work particularly well. It is how a lot of new shows get created today, and that is to come up with a new version of an old idea. This new version would be a reimagining of an old idea, meaning that none of the characters, title, or anything is used from the old idea. It's still considered original but a big advantage in developing this type of show is that you don't need to buy the rights to the old idea because it is a totally different new version. This should not be confused with a 'reboot,' which is an updated version of an old TV show. In this instance, you would need to buy the rights in order to develop it. (*See #2 below*)

When I was working at Spelling Entertainment, AARON SPELLING told us about a show he produced in the 1969, called, *The New People.* It ran on ABC for one season (17 episodes). He had the beta-tapes (pre-video cassette tapes) in storage, which I watched. The show was about a group of survivors of a plane crash on a mysterious island. Sound familiar? It should because there have been several TV shows made that are similar to this idea. We had a show on UPN that we developed based on this idea called, *Mysterious Island*. Then years later, *Lost* was produced on ABC. Now if you take out the element of the plane crash and replace it with a boat, you have *Gilligan's Island*! Similarly, *CSI* is just another way to do an old show called, *Quincy*. *How I met your Mother* is another way to do *Friends*. *Goonies* becomes *Stranger Things* and the list goes on and on.

2. 'INTELLECTUAL PROPERTIES' (IPs)

Ideas can come from intellectual properties. These are ideas based on articles, books, comic books, graphic novels, someone's life rights (past or present), short stories, poems, blogs, past TV shows, movies, or basically any idea for a show that has been published or produced. In order to use these ideas for TV shows you would need to obtain the rights. (*See "How to Option" below*) Examples are *The Walking Dead* (based on a comic book); *Game of Thrones* and *Big, Little Lies* (based on books); *Fargo* (based on a movie); and *One Day at a Time* (based on an old TV show).

3. PUBLIC DOMAIN

An idea can also come from the public domain. These are literary works that are owned by the public and were published before 1923. This means that you do not have to option (make an agreement for the rights) these publications, like you would an IP. An example of this could be anything written by WILLIAM SHAKE-SPEARE. You can also have an idea that is loosely based on historical events, like *Genius*, which aired on NatGeo in 2017. If the IP was written after 1977, it becomes public domain 70 years after the death of the author. Between 1923 and 1977, there are different laws that apply. For works created during that time, refer to the copyright website, Copyright.gov.

HOW TO 'REVERSE ENGINEER' A PROJECT

Let's say you have a great original idea for a TV show. Nowadays it is preferable for buyers, and thus more salable, if your idea is based on your own IP. If you create a comic book or graphic novel based on your original idea before taking it to the market, you can base your series on that IP. This is an example of reverse engineering a project.

Or, let's say you have a great original spec script, but the networks are more interested in buying pitches this season. If you or your producers/studio believes it will sell better as a pitch rather than a spec, then you can reverse engineer it and pitch the concept rather than go out with the spec script.

WHAT ARE THE DIFFERENT FORMATS OF TV SHOWS?

4. Drama

5. Comedy

6. Reality

7. Back-door Pilots

8. Mini-series/Limited series

9. Movies of the Week (MOWs)

10. Anthology series

■ DRAMA

Dramas are usually one-hour in length, however this is changing. For broadcast and basic cable networks, one-hour dramas are actually closer to 42 minutes in order to allow for the commercials. On premium networks (like HBO, Showtime, Starz, and streaming outlets like Netflix and Hulu) there are no commercials and the one-hour drama is around 60 to 85 minutes. I don't believe there will be any episodes of a show that would go longer than that because then it becomes a feature length movie.

Dramas can also be serialized or 'procedural.' Serialized dramas have episodes which are connected and must be watched in order. Some examples are *This is Us*, *The Sopranos* and *Orphan Black*.

Procedural dramas (sometimes called, "franchise") have stand-alone episodes. They do not need to be watched in order. Some examples are *CSI*, *Law and Order* and *House*.

There are also hybrids like *Six Feet Under*, *Nip/Tuck*, *X-Files* and *The Good Wife* where there is a "case" or story of the week, and then on-going storylines that connect each episode.

■ COMEDY

Comedies are usually a half-hour in length. On broadcast and basic cable it is closer to 22 minutes, and on premium and streaming outlets it's closer to 30 minutes. There is also a hybrid comedy/drama, which can either be 30 minutes or a one-hour format and these are called, Dramedies. Comedies can be serialized or not.

■ REALITY

Reality shows vary in length. For example, *The Real World* was a half-hour in length. *Survivor* and *American Idol* are one-hour each with some episodes extending to two-hours in length including commercials.

■ BACK-DOOR PILOTS

Back-door pilots are intended to be first episode to a longer series but in the event they don't do well, they can air it as a two-hour movie. An example of this is the pilot from *Lost* on ABC.

■ MINI-SERIES/LIMITED SERIES

Mini-series/limited series are usually one-hour dramas that are serialized and close-ended after one season. Examples are *Olive*

Kitteridge; Big, Little Lies; and *The Night Of;* all on HBO. Some can continue like *Fargo, American Crime Story,* and *American Horror Story,* but each would have a completely different cast and/or story-line for every season.

■ MOVIES OF THE WEEK (MOWs)

MOWs are movies made especially for television. There weren't many made because most producers wanted it to have a theatrical run before airing it on TV. However, MOWs are making a comeback. Hallmark, Lifetime, HBO and, more recently, Netflix are producing MOWs.

■ ANTHOLOGY SERIES

In an Anthology series, the episodes are connected by an overall theme, yet are stand-alone. They are not serialized and can be watched out of order. Some examples are shows like *Twilight Zone, Tales from the Crypt, Outer Limits* and *Black Mirror.*

Sometimes shows like *Fargo* and *American Horror Story* are referred to as an Anthology Series. In fact, they are more of a hybrid between an Anthology and Limited/Mini-Series because they have a different cast and story-line in each season. A "true Anthology series" would have stand-alone episodes and are only connected by the sweeping "theme" of the series.

HOW DO YOU KNOW IF YOU HAVE A *GOOD* IDEA FOR A TV SHOW?

Whether it's original or comes from an IP, here are some criteria:

Good Ideas For TV:

- Should speak to you, mean something to you, and be something you are passionate about!

- Have character arcs, change over time and possess many stories. In procedurals (dramas that have stand-alone episodes) this is less so, but the characters still should have arcs.

- Are clear and simple to explain yet complicated enough to fill several seasons of stories!

Ideas Not Ideal For A TV Show:

- Work better in a two-hour format/three-act format. They are more of an event, which is something that has changed someone's life in a significant way.

- Works well in short-form, like a web series (2-15 minutes length episodes).

- Are convoluted, confusing and not relatable.

SHOULD YOU PURSUE A PARTICULAR PROJECT?

If you are a writer, producer, director, studio or production company development executive, simply put, you should if:

- You can sell it
- You love it
- You believe in it

If you are a network development executive you should if:

- You believe in it
- It's within your networks' brand
- It will connect with your audience

HOW TO OPTION AN IP AND/OR A SPEC SCRIPT

You do it with a legal, written agreement between you and the rights holder of the material ("Agreement"). In the Agreement, you negotiate the terms of the deal. The standard way to obtain these agreements is through an entertainment attorney.

There are Two Kinds of Agreements:

1. An 'Option Agreement' is where the person proposing the agreement (producer) pays the creator for the rights upfront for his/her material. Everything (credits, points, time, etc.) is negotiated and agreed upon before the producer can present it to the marketplace.

2. A 'Shopping Agreement' is where there is no upfront cost for the person proposing for the agreement (the producer). They have the right to "shop" (try to sell) the project for "x" amount of time for no upfront cost. Then the studio or network that buys the project will make deals with both the producer and the creator of the IP.

What are the Benefits and/or Costs of an Option Agreement?

- The benefit of an Option Agreement to the creator is that she or he will not have to wait to get paid for their project (IP). The benefit to the producers is that since they paid for the rights upfront, they will get more in return. The length of time they have to sell the project, the 'points' on the back-end (profit sharing), and the fees that both parties would get on the project once it is sold will be pre-negotiated and, of course, in the producer's favor.

- The cost of an Option Agreement to the creator is that she or he will not get the best deal for their project (IP). Waiting to make a deal with the studio, puts the creator in the power position. The cost for the producers is that it literally costs them cash out-of-pocket.

What are the Benefits and/or Costs of a Shopping Agreement?

- A Shopping Agreement is beneficial for the producers as well as the creators/rights' holders. It's good for the producers because they don't have to put any money up in order to be attached to the project (IP). It is good for the creator because, once the project (IP) is sold, she or he will make a better deal with the studio directly.

- The cost of a Shopping Agreement for the creator is that she or he will not get any money until it is sold. The cost for the producer is that she or he may not get as great a deal once the project is sold than if they had paid for the rights prior to selling it.

YOU HAVE A GREAT IDEA. NOW WHAT?

PROTECT IT!

The most commonly used methods by professionals today is by registering with the Library of Congress or the Writers Guild of America's (WGA) time-stamped registration for proof of creation. You will receive an instant WGA Registration number when registering online, and a certificate by mail to follow.

■ Copyright Basics

The United States copyright law gives the creator(s) of said works exclusive claim of ownership over their work. In addition to legal protection, copyright protection encourages respect for the creators and for their ideas. It provides exclusive claim of ownership to the copyright holder and they may allow their works to be used by other parties without fear that their ideas will not be attributed to them.

It should be noted that you cannot copyright an "idea." You need to have a script or at least an outline/treatment for the idea. For reality show ideas, you can put together a treatment that explains the idea and format of the show.

YOU HAVE PROTECTED AND/OR OPTIONED A PROJECT. NOW WHAT?

If you are the writer, or you have a writer attached to your project, you should begin working on the pitch and putting together the 'package' and strategy for the project. I will get more into that in the below. (*See "Strategies for Selling a TV Show" in Act 3*)

If you don't have a writer, and you just acquired the rights to an IP, start thinking about how to adapt it into a series. When you are meeting with writers, or if you can set up a meeting with producers, production companies, studios or networks, you will need to pitch how you believe the IP can work as a series.

To start looking for writers you should put together, what is known in TV Development as, a 'writers list.' You may find this to be one of your most often-executed tasks since you will need a list for every project and it has to be updated all the time. But it is an integral part of the process for success and you will find this to be one of your most useful tools.

WHAT, WHY AND HOW DO YOU PUT TOGETHER A WRITERS LIST?

WHAT is a Writers List?

*   Let's say you are a producer in need of a writer for your project. You would put together this "wish" list, keeping in mind that these writers should be obtainable; meaning they are potentially available when you would need them and would be open to listening to your idea(s).

Act 2

WHY would you put a Writers List together?

- You will produce a list for every project you have in development for two important reasons: First, to find a writer for the project; second, if your show gets on the air you would need to staff it with writers, and once the show is on the air, you will have on-going staffing needs.

- Another list of writers to create is with those you've read. Whether you want to be a development executive, writer, producer or director it will be useful to keep a list of your thoughts on every script you read. If you are an assistant, you may need to make a list of the writers your boss has read. Knowing writers and keeping a writers lists will prove to be invaluable for your future as an entertainment professional

HOW do you put a Writers List together for a specific project?

- First, you can look through the TV shows currently being produced/on the air that are similar to your project and see who the writers are on that show.

- Also, in general, if you develop a show with lower-level writers you will need to attach a showrunner. This is because the networks are not only buying ideas, they are also buying experienced people who can produce the show for them. Lower-level writers are learning and, once they've worked their way up on numerous shows, networks will be eager to work with them. Showrunners are in need all the time. This is a very highly coveted job in the TV industry. You can find this information on IMDBpro.com or on the shows (in the credits) themselves.

- Another way to put together a writers list is, if you are an executive you will most likely be getting submissions from agents. You will need to read these scripts in order to decide which writer makes the most sense for your project.

The format of writers lists vary, but it should include the following:

- name of the writer
- his or her agent
- contact information
- best and current credits (including the last title, ie., EP, co-EP)
- a section for notes (where you can include what happened when pursuing them, or not, etc.)

A writers list is an extremely important part of the development process.

Let's say you have successfully put together a writers list, pursued several writers and attached the best one for your project. Great job!

YOU HAVE A WRITER. WHAT'S THE NEXT STEP?

The all important PITCH.

When pitching the show, the writer and/or creator will discuss his or her idea for the pilot script as well as the series. Whether you are working with a studio or planning to pitch the idea to them, you would work on a 'pitch document.'

At this point, you should decide if you want to develop this idea into a script before pitching it. This can be done independently or with a studio. The different ways to develop a script from an original concept or an IP will be covered below. (*See "Script Development"*)

If you choose to develop the script, after it is completed you would be pitching the long arc of the series in order to sell it to a network (*See "Goal of Network Pitch #2" below*) or to try and get independent financing. (*See "Indie TV" in Act 3*)

In this section, I discuss the different aspects of pitching, the pitch document, how to work on one, the importance of it for your pitch, and the pitch itself!

THE NETWORK PITCH

There are two kinds of pitches:

- Selling an idea to get a script order (and possibly more)

- Selling a spec script to get a series order

THREE WAYS TO GET A PITCH MEETING WITH A NETWORK

1. If you have an agent and/or studio attached to your project they will set up the meeting for you.

2. If you know the network executives, you can call and set up the meetings yourself.

3. You can 'cold call'. A cold call is when you don't know the executives, but you call them to inform them about your project and try to set up a meeting. If you have an IP the network is interested in, they will probably meet with you even if you don't have TV credits.

During your phone conversation, you will have a brief chance to get them interested/excited about your project. This is sometimes referred to as the "elevator pitch," and is very different than the formal meeting done at the network. On this call, they will make sure they don't have something similar in development, the show has a concept they are interested in developing, and is one they feel is right for their brand. *(See "Know the Audience" in Act 3)* If the network is interested, they will set up a more formal meeting where the writer pitches the idea more in depth about the idea.

Who are the Participants in a Network Pitch Meeting?

- Writer/creator(s) (which could be a showrunner as well)
- Showrunner
- Producer(s)
- Talent (if attached)
- Studio executives (if attached)
- Agent(s) (sometimes, not always)
- And of course, the network executive(s)

WHAT IS THE GOAL OF YOUR NETWORK PITCH?

1. If you are selling an idea to get a "pilot script order" (and hopefully more), you are coming in with a concept/idea/IP that you will pitch in order to get the network to buy the pilot script or, even better, a series order which would be written by the writer you have attached to your project.

2. If you are meeting with the network after they've read and liked a spec that you've sent them, you are now pitching them to get a series order. This is a totally different kind of pitch. In this case, you are selling them on where the series is going (the long arc of the series, which could include up to five seasons), what the themes are, what statement you are trying to make, etc. But, if it's a limited series it could have any number of episodes from 6-13. Also, if you have a plan to have that limited series go on for additional seasons like *Fargo*. (*See Pitch Document based on a Spec Script below*)

WHAT IS A 'BIBLE' FOR A TV SERIES?

As you prepare for your pitch, you should work on the bible for the show. You wouldn't necessarily pitch the whole bible, but it's good to have most of it thought out. The bible is the extended plan for the series. Whether it is a comedy or drama, serialized or a franchise (procedural), it would include:

1. Logline
2. Description of the 'world'/Overview of the series
3. Themes
4. Tone
5. Main character descriptions

For a Procedural/Franchise show:

The bible would include many episode ideas because the network needs to see that the show can last, at least a hundred episodes!

For a Serialized show:

The bible would include detailed arcs for the main characters and story in the first season, along with ideas for season two and beyond. The network would want to understand and see that you have a clear vision of the show's first season. Also, make sure to add REVEALS along the way and a BIG TWIST in the finale, that propels the viewer into season two.

WHAT IS A PITCH DOCUMENT?

Now that you know who you are pitching to and what you are pitching, how do you properly prepare for the pitch?

A Pitch Document is a blueprint for the pitch. The writer/creator of the show and the producers work together on this document. If there is a studio involved, initially they would *not* work on it, but would get involved after the producers are ready to share it with them (studio executives).

Writers and producers use this document as a tool for preparing the pitch before pitching to the networks. If all goes well at the studio run-through, the producer and/or writer would then perfect it with the studio's input.

Your pitch should always consist of these four elements from which you will expand upon: The IDEA, the WORLD, the CHARACTERS and the STORYLINES.

THE PITCH DOCUMENT BASED ON AN IDEA:

This idea can be original, an IP or from the Public Domain, and should contain the following elements:

- The opening (or the first thing to consider) is how the writer/ creator, plan to start the pitch. For example, you can open with the proposed beginning of the pilot (like the teaser, which is the opening scene), or you can open with a description of the main character. You can use the set-up, the themes, or the world of the show.

- Another important element is a logline, which is a short de-scription of the show that includes the format and world. For example, "This is a single-camera, half-hour comedy about..."

- Perhaps the most important consideration in any of the above scenarios is, "Is it engaging?" "Does it draw people in?"

There are many different ways to start your pitch. Deciding what works best for you and your idea is crucial.

- Next, the writer can describe the overview, or premise of the show. This is where the creator can get into more of the details that are part of the bible (where the series will live, what the world of the show is, the tone, look, etc.).

- At this point, the writer can go into more detail about the characters, their descriptions, arcs, turns, reveals, themes, etc. What is unique and unusual about these character or world?

- Once again, it is most important to be engaging throughout the pitch. Enrapt your audience in your vision and take them on a journey. Paint a visual story they can "see" on the TV screen. It should not be memorized but known inside and out!

There are some writers who post pitch documents online. You may be able to access these samples on the internet.

If a network has read and liked your spec pilot script, you will not have to pitch as outlined above.

THE PITCH DOCUMENT BASED ON A SPEC SCRIPT:

Your pitch should be focused on the following:

- Getting into the details included in your bible of the series.

- The network will be very interested in finding out specifically what happens in episode two and beyond. This would include all character arcs, storylines, plot twists and turns, etc.

THREE IMPORTANT QUESTIONS TO ANSWER IN YOUR PITCH

This holds true whether you are trying to sell an idea or after they've read your spec pilot.

1. WHY YOU? Why are you the perfect person for this project? Talk about what attracted you to this project and how it resonates with you.

2. WHY NOW? Why is it perfect timing for this project? Talk about why it is relevant in the marketplace and at this point in time. Does it have any relevance to what is happening in the world now or projected to happen? Does it have social or political relevance?

3. WHY SHOULD WE CARE? Explain why we should care about this show. What is the series saying to its audience? Why does this need to be a series?

For either type of pitch, one last thing you may want to discuss is the network's audience and how it would resonate with them.

HOW TO TELL A GOOD PITCH FROM A NOT-SO-GOOD PITCH

A Good Pitch:

- Is engaging
- Keeps them interested
- Has them asking probing questions

A Not-So-Good Pitch:

- They are checking their watches
- Their eyes are glazed over, yawning
- They are not looking at you
- They are asking questions about things you already discussed
- They said they are not getting it or that they are confused

WHAT HAPPENS AFTER THE PITCH?

If the network buys your project "in the room," it literally means they said at the end of the meeting they want it.

CONGRATULATIONS! You've done a perfect job!

THE NETWORK ORDERS A PILOT PRESENTATION

This means that the network has ordered a shorter version of the pilot episode. There are various reasons why a network might do this. It could be that they really like the idea, but aren't one hundred percent sure if it would work for them, or it could be they want to see how it plays with the actors, or financial reasons, etc.

THE NETWORK DOESN'T BUY IT IN THE ROOM

This is by far the more common occurrence, do not despair. Unless they say otherwise, you are in the running. Most of the time they need to discuss it internally before making a decision.

It is true that you will probably not sell your show in the room. However, there are many factors that could affect their decision, such as fitting in with their brand (the network), what they currently have in development, how they are doing financially, if they have a new top executive who wants to change their mandate, etc. These are just a few of the variables that can affect the acceptance of your project. Also, take note, you may sell it days, weeks or even months after the pitch meeting, In other words, don't give up on your project!

Words to live by when pitching a show: **IT ONLY TAKES ONE YES!**

WHAT ARE THE STANDARD VS. NEWER WAYS OF PITCHING?

STANDARD WAY (OLD SCHOOL):

- Writers come to the networks and verbally pitch their shows. This would include a general story for the pilot with examples of episodes and an overall tone and theme of the series.

NEW WAYS (NEW SCHOOL):

- Today, spec pilot scripts are being submitted directly to the networks, and sometimes even with one or two more episodes included in the bible for the series.

- The use of visual aids during a pitch, such as posters, blown-up pictures, sizzle reels and video presentations, are becoming more prevalent. With animation projects it's almost a given to have some artwork or a reel showing the look you are pitching.

- There are so many outlets today with very different brands, so networks look for something that is specifically for them.

WHAT IS A SIZZLE REEL?

A sizzle reel is a video presentation for the pitch of your project. Do you need one? Possibly, but not always. For a reality pitch, the answer is yes. But, for scripted shows, you will need to decide if the potential benefits outweigh the potential risks in your particular case.

POTENTIAL BENEFITS:

- It can evoke the tone of the show, which might be an important part of your show and something you want to emphasize.

- It can visually stimulate your meeting, so that the network executives are not just sitting there listening.

- If your idea is hard to convey with a verbal pitch, a sizzle reel may be your answer.

- Visual aids are also good when a project has many characters or a lot of details that could get lost due to time constraints.

POTENTIAL RISKS:

- If the network executives don't like it, it can hurt or ruin your presentation. This can result from a variety of issues, such as poor production value, bad acting, not portraying your idea very well, etc.

- It is a limited way of expressing your idea and may not display the true way you wish to convey your project.

- When your reel is over, it can mean your chances are over. You have to try not to shoot yourself in the foot. Remember it is important to make sure the reel satisfies your reasons for producing it.

Act 2

HOW DO YOU MAKE A SIZZLE REEL?

If you decide a reel will help your presentation, here are some ways to put one together.

1. You can produce (pay for) it with your own money.

2. Ask your friends to help you for free or for very little money.

3. You can literally grab video footage from online and edit it together.

4. You can make a video collage of photos and add text to the screen to tell your story.

YOU'VE PITCHED YOUR SHOW AND IT DIDN'T SELL. NOW WHAT?

DO NOT GIVE UP!

Here are a couple of reasons that may explain why you didn't sell your show beyond the obvious, like the pitch didn't go well.

1. Timing is everything. This plays a huge factor. Let's say you have a project about a serial killer. Not just any serial killer, but one we've never heard, seen or could have imagined. Now just as you are about to go out and pitch your idea, a story breaks out about a real life killer that is eerily similar. Even though you can show you were working on this project long before these crimes were committed, it would never sell because buyers would think it's in poor taste to the families of the victims to do a show so soon. However, if you wait several years, doing this show would not only be totally possible, but even probable. Many shows are taken from real life, but timing is everything. Current events can also affect your show. For example, you could have a scenario in your show that in-

cludes a devastating natural disaster. If that happens in real life, you, the studio, and the network may decide the timing is not right to run the show/episode. This does happen and will continue to happen because art imitates life (and vice versa).

2. The network says they have a project that is similar to yours in development. This is a tough one because it feels and sounds like the network can say this and then just go ahead and steal your idea. In my experience, they don't. They would have to participate in a cover-up and hope they aren't sued. On the other hand, it is true that people are pitching shows all the time. It would indeed be rare that your show is so unique that no one else is pitching, or has pitched something similar.

YOU HAVE PITCHED AND SOLD YOUR IDEA! WHAT'S THE NEXT STEP?

SCRIPT DEVELOPMENT

If you were thinking it's all about the pitch, of course the pitch is crucial otherwise you would not get to this stage of development. But without a "great script," there is no TV show. Even if you, the producer, and all of your friends, think you have a great script, "great" is a relative term. As discussed earlier, who is to say what is great? In television, it's the NETWORK.

If the network thinks it's great, it is great. It's your job, whether you are a writer, producer, development executive, agent or manager, to champion the project until the head of the network believes it is great. Then your script will become a show.

The development of a script is so important that it is a major factor in getting your show produced. The quality and focus of your script can prove to be the real beginning, or potential end, of your project.

WHAT IS A 'SPEC SCRIPT'?

Spec Scripts are scripts written by writers who did not get paid or commissioned to write the script.

There are two types of spec scripts:

1. One that is based on an original idea
2. One that is based on an episode of an existing show

WHY DO WRITERS WRITE SPEC SCRIPTS?

Writers write original spec scripts to show a sample of their work. It is an opportunity for them to express themselves creatively and it should be unique. It is also a way for producers and executives of networks and studios to see the writer's "voice" (which is unique to every writer) and vision of a proposed new TV show.

Writers write a spec script of an existing TV series to show the executive producers, the creator and showrunner of that show that they can execute an episode in a superb way. It's important that it stands out. So if you are planning to write one, make sure it is a fantastic episode of that show. It should showcase your talent by capturing the essence and voice of the show. This is the typical way for a writer to get a job as a 'staff writer' on a show. It's like a writer's version of an actor going on an audition.

WHAT IS 'COVERAGE' OF A SCRIPT OR BOOK?

Coverage is a report of the script or book that agents, managers, producers or executives get from 'readers' before, or instead of, reading the script or book themselves.

Readers are paid to read a script or book and send in a report similar to a book report. The reader can be an assistant or lower level executive or an outside freelance reader.

The format includes:

- The logline (which is one or two lines about the project)
- Character breakdown
- Synopsis
- Comments
- A "pass" (doesn't want) or "consider" (does want) recommendation.

For a writer or producer, getting good coverage on your script can be extremely beneficial. It will usually get agents and/or managers to help you.

HOW AN IDEA BECOMES A SCRIPT

The following applies to writers working with a studio and/or network attached. For independent development, see "*Indie Developers*" below.

This is the seven-step process an idea goes through to become a script:

1. Story Area
2. Outline
3. First Draft
4. Notes
5. Second Draft
6. Notes
7. Final Draft

1. 'Story Area'

As we explored in the last chapter, the idea or concept can come from the writer, development executive, network executive, an IP, or anyone.

Act 2

After a network commissions your script, the first step is to present the general story area of the pilot episode, which should be a few paragraphs or, at most, a page.

2. Outline

This is a very detailed document where the writer elaborates substantially about the pilot episode. The format for a one-hour broadcast network and basic cable outline consists of the teaser plus acts one through five, scene by scene. In the 1990s, when I started working in this business, TV shows had four acts; one every 15 minutes. It was modeled this way to make room for commercials. There is question if this will change in the future.

Here's how it works:

The teaser leads you into the first commercial break. Act one lasts about 15 to 18 minutes. Act two gets you to around the half-hour mark/commercial break. Act three and four break up the last half hour. Act five is usually a short act at the end that will have a big reveal. This will end the story of that episode, or it will have a big twist that propels you on to the next episode.

Several years ago the networks decided to change this format, adjusting the start and stop times of shows. This way, viewers didn't even realize they were watching the network's next show. It worked, so they have all adapted this new five-act structure.

> *Side note: When I was young viewer, I would get frustrated with the commercial breaks. At that time, of course I didn't know why there were commercials, so I would change the channel hoping to watch another show. But I found that the competing shows ran their commercials at the same time! I used think, "Why don't they run them at different times so people can watch more than one show?" I know now they didn't want viewers to be able to watch other programs so they planned to have breaks at the same time.*

But television is ever-changing. With new technology, including the invention of the DVR, viewers can now watch shows whenever they want completely devoid of commercials.

Over the years, I have found that even though the outline gives more detailed information about the show, there is a fine line as to how much to give. This document must include every scene you plan to have in your pilot; however you don't want to get bogged down in the minutia. There are some times when less is more.

It is also important to remember that outlines are sales documents and should be treated as such. You don't want to un-sell the project before it even becomes a script.

When the writer is done with the outline, she or he will submit it to the producer to get their notes before handing it to the studio attached to the project. Then, when everyone is happy, it is submitted to the network.

It is not uncommon, even after getting notes from the network executive(s), for them to change their minds. Trying to please them is often futile, but you have to keep in mind that they are your buyer. You should do your best to stay true to the show's vision, but be collaborative and inclusive with the studio and/or network. Remember, it doesn't matter where good ideas for your show come from as long as it keeps the momentum going and improves the show.

FOR INDIE DEVELOPERS:

If you are an independent producer, or a development executive for a producer who is working directly with a writer without a studio, it is ideal if the writer is willing to give you an outline before writing the script. (That is, if the writer is not being compensated. If she or he is being compensated, it will probably be included in the deal). This will help to avoid unnecessary rewrites of the script.

If you are the writer, I would encourage you to not skip this step. Some writers are so excited about their script that they feel this may be an un-necessary step. But, on the contrary, it is absolutely critical. Imagine if you wrote the entire script only to discover that it doesn't work and you don't know why.

By doing this detailed outline, you will get a blueprint of your script that can be easily revised at this stage. After the script is written, it will be much harder and more tedious to rework. It's like building a house with-out first doing the blueprints.

Once everyone is happy with the outline, the writer can move on to the third step of the process.

3. First Draft

This is the first pass of the pilot script for the TV series.

It is first sent to the producer, if one is attached. It is the produc-er's job to give the writer feedback on how to make the script bet-ter. If there is no producer attached, it will go directly to the stu-dio. They will give notes to the writer before this first draft is sent to the network.

It is not unusual for writers to rewrite their first draft several times before sending it into the studio and/or network.

4. Notes

This is the step in the process when the network gives notes to the writer.

I would like to point out that since the producer and/or studio already gave the writer their notes before the first draft was hand-ed in to the network, they would not want to give more notes at this point because they wouldn't want to overwhelm the writer. This is the time for the network to give their thoughts (notes). If indeed the producer and/or studio have further suggestions, they would not tell the writer until after they receive the network's notes. They would not give the writer any more notes during the phone call or the meeting with the network.

Once the writer receives the notes from the network executives, the writer can proceed to the fifth step in the process.

FOR INDIE DEVELOPERS:

The producer gives notes to the writer after receiving the first draft. If the producer finds many, or significant, structural changes/thoughts, then they might suggest the writer do another outline. It may save time in the long run because you can see if the changes will track before the writer makes the shifts within the draft.

5. Second Draft

Once the writer hands in this important second draft, it is the producer's job to make sure the writer included and executed the network's notes. When the producers/studio feel it is ready to share with the network, they will send it in.

It is quite possible for the writer to go through another couple of more drafts at this stage. If all is going well, the script is improving and moving forward. Your TV show is getting closer to being realized.

The second draft is now submitted to the network. The writer, producer and studio all await word from the network.

6. Notes

This step is the network's last chance to weigh in and give any other thoughts about the script before getting the last, most important version of the script. Before submitting the final draft to the network, the producer and the studio have one last chance to give the writer any more thoughts about changes to the script.

FOR INDIE DEVELOPERS:

The producer gives the writer his or her thoughts about this revised second draft.

7. Final Draft

This final draft is the one that the writer, the producer, studio and network executives should be most proud of and excited about. It is the vision of the show in its realized scripted form. It is the beginning.

If your script is good enough, and the timing is right, you will find out if your project will be produced, find a life, and exist beyond the pages. This draft is the essence of your TV show.

FOR INDIE DEVELOPERS:

This final draft is the one the writer and producer are most satisfied with and excited to send out to the networks.

HOW DO PRODUCERS AND EXECUTIVES GIVE NOTES?

The cardinal rule is to first tell the writer what you *like* the most about the script! Lay out what is working, and then you can get into all your other thoughts and concerns. After you talk about all that the writer accomplished well, you would then go over the script in this order:

1. Overview and general notes (What is this script about? What can be done to make it resonate better?)

2. Tone (Is it a campy or straight forward show?)
3. Character notes/concerns (This includes the arcs, descriptions, etc.)

4. Plot (Does the story move forward? What are the reveals?)

5. 'Page notes' and Typos (small notes you have on a page)

> *Side note: People often ask me the difference between good writers and great writers. I believe good writers can write fantastic first drafts, but great writers are able to make good use of the notes they receive. They are open to constructive criticism and can adjust their work to make it better.*

HELPFUL NOTES VS. HARMFUL NOTES

HELPFUL NOTES

The most important and useful way to give notes is being able to communicate your thoughts without offending the writer. Some ways to be constructive are:

- Ask for clarification if you don't understand what the writer is trying to convey.

- Ask to understand the motivation for a character on something that she or he is doing.

- Give examples on how to fix the problem that you are bringing up. Remember you are a team.

- Ask, don't tell. Discuss your thoughts.

HARMFUL NOTES

If there is something in the script that isn't working for you, tell the writer in a non-threatening and constructive way.

Examples that can hurt the process:

1. When giving notes for a comedy script, don't say that something is not funny. Most of the time with comedies, how the actor says his or her lines will make all the difference as to

what is funny or not. Also, humor is extremely subjective. Funny to one person may not be funny to another.

2. Being general and not specific will *not* help the writer. It's important to start with general concerns but, in order to get your point across, you will need to follow up with very specific examples.

3. Never tell a writer to change something just because you say so. It is important to remember that this is their show, their vision. Your job is to let them know if they are not getting that vision across to readers.

4. Be clear in your points. The more the writer can understand the issues you are bringing up the better. In order for the writer to be able to make adjustments to the script, she or he has to completely appreciate the problem(s) you are having.

Both you and the writer do not have to have the entire solution figured out at this point. Many times, the writer will need to take some time to figure out how to change it.

*****

Act 2

Assignments

Get your hands on a script! Where to find one? You can get samples at your local library and the Writers Guild of America's (WGA) offices. You can ask your friends, relatives, co-workers, and even find them online. They are out there.

Read the script and make your notes on it. Work to improve it.

If the script is really good you may find it hard to come up with notes. Don't force it. Sometimes it is harder *not* to give notes and appreciate a good script for what it is.

Other times a script can be way off base and you don't even know where to start. Refer back to the section, 'How Do Producers and Executives Give Notes,' which will give you the tools. It's always best to start with the bigger, more general thoughts and concerns, and then make your way to the specifics notes. Also always give examples when giving notes in order to explain it better.

Write your thoughts down as if you were going to give them to the writer. Writing down your notes will force you to be clear about what you are saying. Also, it will come out better than if you said it directly to the writer because you will have time to adjust it, make it more clear, etc.

After you've done that, see if you can give these ideas and thoughts to the writer. Find out if you are able to convey your ideas in a way that make sense to the writer. Did the writer agree with all or any of your notes? Did she or he argue with you? Did she or he have good points that counter your notes? Did you feel after the session that the script is going to get better?

If the writer does another draft of the script, you may be able to tell if your notes made it better. But remember that sometimes, if the script doesn't get better, it doesn't mean your notes weren't good. It could mean that the writer did not understand what was not working for you, or maybe you thought it was one issue but it turned out to be something else. These are common reasons why many times a great idea does not go past the script phase of development. It is heart-breaking because so much work and thought is put into a project and it just doesn't get there.

It's important to keep at it. Don't give up!

As long as the writer is passionate and willing to work on it, the producer should as well. Keep thinking of the old adage, "The show must go on!"

*****

ACT THREE

The Market Place

THE NETWORKS

In every field there are buyers and sellers. As the writer or producer of a TV script/idea for a TV series, or even the director or
actor attached to the project, you are the seller. The networks are
the buyers. It is where your ideas for your show will find its
home, come alive and belong. This chapter examines the importance of understanding how the networks operate and what they
are looking for.

THE BUYERS:

Here is the current list of outlets that are actively buying scripted
content at the time of this printing:

**ABC, APPLE, ADULT SWIM, AMAZON, AMC, AUDIENCE,
BBCA, BET, BRAVO, CBS, CBS: ALL ACCESS, CINEMAX,**

COMEDY CENTRAL, CRACKLE, CW, DISCOVERY, DISNEY, DISNEY JR., DISNEY+, E!, EL REY, EPIX, FACEBOOK, THE NEW FOX, FREEFORM, FX, FXX, HBO, HBO MAX, HISTORY, HULU, IFC, LIFETIME, LOGO, MTV, NATGEO, NBC, NETFLIX, NICKELODEON, NICK JR., OWN, PARAMOUNT, PEACOCK (NBC streaming service), SHOWTIME, STARZ, STAGE 13, SUNDANCE, SYFY, TBS, TNT, USA, WE TV

As you can see, there are a plethora of places to sell your project.

KNOW THE AUDIENCE AND THE NETWORK

The two most important factors to learn when researching buyers are:

1. Who is their audience?
2. What is their brand?

These distinctions will inform you as to where to take your project. Knowing the demographics of your show and the demographics the network wants to reach will be a great help in leading you to your goal. Understanding what shows each network currently develops and the differences between them will also guide you.

In the last 20 years, the number of U.S. television buyers, or outlets, went from 6 to over 50! Therefore, it is important to start by creating a list for yourself so you can keep track of all the buyers and their audiences. I call it the 'Buyers List.' Every development executive and/or producer will have a version of this list in general, and then they will generate one for each project.

> *Side note: It is not easy to get a handle on more than 50 places that are looking for content. Oftentimes they are moving targets. Once you think you understand what they want, they go and change their brand! Also, there are currently three outlets that are targeting all demographics. They are Netflix, Amazon and*

Apple.   These companies have separate departments that cover the different groups.   Navigating and knowing who to pitch to has become quite the challenge.

WHAT IS A BUYERS LIST?

The Buyers List is a list of all the networks, channels, and streaming outlets. You should consider a buyer anyone who will pay for content to air.

You can decide what elements to include on your spreadsheet/table, but the basics should have the following:

1. The name of the network, e.g., ABC, FX, Netflix, or HBO.

2. Contact information. The name of the development executive you would call to discuss your project.

3. Brand/Mandate information.   This is a brief description of who is watching that network and their types of programming, e.g., for SYFY- more male than female 18 to 49, genre/science-fiction.

4. Notes section.   This section can include your thoughts about which of your projects you would like to present, what happened when you called, when you met, etc.

By exploring which buyers are looking for what kind of shows, and why, it will help you plan and strategize where to sell your projects. (*See "Strategy" below*)

ARE THERE ANY DIFFERENCES SELLING TO A BROADCAST NETWORK, A STREAMING PLATFORM, A PREMIUM CABLE OR BASIC CABLE CHANNEL?

Yes, definitely. Here's how it breaks down.

Act 3

BROADCAST NETWORKS:

ABC, CBS, The NEW FOX, NBC, CW

They transmit to everyone with a television at no cost to the viewer because the content is paid for by advertisers. That's why there are so many commercials.

When selling to Broadcast Networks and Basic Cable vs. Premium Cable and Streaming platforms, it is important to consider the format of your show. Broadcast and Basic Cable shows have 'act breaks' to allow for commercials and it is standard that they end in cliffhangers. The network is hoping that viewers believe they will miss something important if they change the channel and are persuaded to stay tuned through the commercials.

On the other hand, Streaming services have no act breaks in their TV shows per se. They may have an end of a scene that feels like the perfect time to go to a commercial, but they don't. They continue on to the next scene.

Even though all TV outlets have their own rights to self-censorship, some are more tightly regulated than others. Broadcast Networks act in accordance to rules called, 'Standards and Practices.' This is a department at the network that is governed by federal regulations and determines if a show can air. It includes looking at all moral, ethical or legal implications that the program may infer onto the network. This can include what they consider to be "mature language," "sexual content," etc. These Standards and Practices have an obligation to protect the public since the programming is free and easily accessible to all, especially children. With Broadcast channels there is less of a need for viewer discretion.

With Basic Cable there are also Standards and Practices in place, however their rules are more relaxed. The thought is that because this service is not free and you have to pay for it, it is more likely mom and dad will regulate what the kids are watching.

Streaming/Internet outlets have parental controls which can be selected and activated to control viewing. This is why there are no Standards and Practices rules in place for these channels.

BASIC CABLE:

ADULT SWIM, AMC, BET, BBCA, COMEDY CENTRAL, DIS-NEY, DISNEY JR., DISCOVERY, E!, FREEFORM, FX, FXX, HALLMARK, IFC, LIFETIME, MTV, NATGEO, NICK-ELODEON, NICK JR., OWN, PARAMOUNT, SUNDANCE, SYFY, TNT, USA, WE TV

When these Basic Cable networks started, they had to figure out how to compete with the "Big Six" (this is what we called the broadcast networks in the 1990s because it included UPN and the WB). Before most of them made a name for themselves, HBO (*a Premium Cable network, defined below*) found its audience. Other Basic Cable networks soon followed suit. They realized they had to be different and find theirs as well. One by one, most of them have found their niche. In 2017, there were about 94 million Cable TV subscribers. (*Variety*, *"Cord-Cutting Soared in 2017"*)

When the programming is not working, or there is a shift in executives, the heads of the network may change their brand. They hire a whole new development team, restructure and try again. Some examples are ABCFamily became FREEFORM; UPN and WB became the CW; and SPIKE is now PARAMOUNT.

PREMIUM CABLE/STREAMING:

APPLE, AMAZON PRIME VIDEO, CINEMAX, CBS: ALL AC-CESS, DISNEY+, EPIX, FACEBOOK, HBO, HBO MAX, HULU, LOGO, NETFLIX, PEACOCK, SHOWTIME, STAGE 13, STARZ, AWESOMENESS

Premium Cable/Streaming services work differently than Broadcast or Basic Cable because the viewer is charged a subscription fee. These outlets don't have to rely on money from advertisers/

commercials, ratings or Standards and Practices. All they care about is selling subscriptions.

In order for them to stand out, they produce shows that would never be allowed to air on Broadcast or Basic Cable networks. In 2017, HBO had 54 million subscribers in the US alone. (*Statista.com* *"Number of HBO Domestic Subscribers"* 2017)

In the last five to eight years, the Streaming/online networks took this same model and created their own channels. At first, everyone wasn't sure if it was going to work. Streaming content over the internet was very, very slow. Nowadays, it's almost seamless and they are able to compete. It seems every day there is a new website creating original content. In 2017, Netflix had over 55 million subscribers in the US alone. "For comparison, there are about 94 million pay TV subscribers in the U.S."(*Recode.com,* *"Netflix Now Has Nearly 118 Million Streaming Subscribers Globally,"* 2017)

WHAT IS THE FUTURE OF THE BROADCAST AND CABLE NETWORKS?

There are many people who believe Broadcast networks will not be around forever and will one day be replaced. That is a real possibility. It is also what the subscription-based networks/channels would like you to believe, as that is their competition.

Today, there are mergers and much consolidation in the media business. Recently Disney bought much of FOX because they wanted a bigger stake in Hulu. This is causing major changes in the system. Most of us do not know how this will all shake out, but my feeling is that this will change the Broadcast and Basic Cable channels' future.

Also, there is a current trend by some families to "cut the cord" and not pay for cable TV. There's the thought that, in the future, the TV and computer will become one and the same. I believe in order for this to happen, Streaming will have to become as visually clear as the Cable networks' productions. Although the quality of streaming video nowadays has vastly improved, at times it leaves much to be desired. Once the quality is there, I still believe there will be a need for live TV. Even as I write this book, Hulu and Amazon Fire have added live TV! Hulu was the first Streaming channel to include a live service. It remains to be seen how it will all play out. Stay tuned...

DO ALL NETWORKS OWN THE CONTENT (SHOWS) ON THEIR CHANNEL?

The answer is sometimes.

- If a network's sister studio *is* attached to produce the series, then they own the show.

- If the show is a co-production between two studios, then both studios own the show.

- If the network is not attached as the studio, they do not own the show. In essence, they are just paying to air the show for a period of time. The Studio that produced the show, owns the show. (*See "The Studios" below*)

DO ALL NETWORKS PRODUCE ORIGINAL CONTENT?

The answer is no.

- There are some networks that have only 'acquired content.' These shows have previously aired on another network. They do not have any original shows, only re-runs of other shows.

- However, more and more channels are realizing that they can make more money by producing original content, so today there are very few networks that only acquire TV content. Some examples are MeTV, WGN, ion, and StartTV.

- Most networks that have original content also have acquired programming.

WHAT IS A LICENSE FEE?

When your show goes into production at a network, the network will pay a fee, per episode, to the studio that is producing it for the rights to air it. This is called a license fee. It is similar to leasing. They are renting the series for a period of time from the studio that owns the show.

HOW DO STUDIOS FIT INTO THE PICTURE?

The studios are companies that own TV shows. Due to the fact that many TV shows cost more money to produce than the networks are willing to pay, studios will deficit finance, or pay, the amount of money it costs to produce it above the network's license fee. This is why they *own* the show. By owning it, they get to sell it domestically, as well as internationally, after the original network airs the show in first-run.

Every time the studio sells that episode, they make money. It's like creating a painting for one gallery to show for a period of time, for a specific price, and then you get it back to sell over and over again to other places. You've done the work one time, yet you make money on it again and again.

Today, more and more networks are working towards owning more of their shows. As discussed earlier, the FCC made rules against this because it became very difficult for independent companies to get their shows produced. A big difference today is that certain outlets, mostly streaming, are making their networks the "go-to" place for independent producers and writers. They are offering creative freedom that independents would not get at traditional networks and, in turn, the outlet gets to own the show.

The downside for independent producers is they don't get the back-end profits that producers received yesteryear. In today's market, a producer, like AARON SPELLING, would have a very different deal than he had back then. At that time, he owned all the shows he produced for the broadcast networks and received a significant amount of the back-end profits. That scenario doesn't happen anymore.

On YouTube, Indie producers can create their own YouTube channel, but they are getting money the more traditional way - through advertisers.

It's possible that one day soon with the success of the streaming platforms that investors will finance independent producers for online content much more than they do today because of the huge profits that can be made with owning TV shows.

"LET'S MAKE A DEAL"

When you hear, "Let's make a deal," from a network and/or studio, you know you've made it! You have beaten the odds and are on your way. This means they are moving forward with your project and/or want to work with you. However, it doesn't guarantee that your show will get made, or even be on the air, but getting a deal is the first step in the right direction! Writers and producers who have at least one, if not more, successful show on the air will most likely get offered a deal.

If you do get your show on the air, it will have to be a hit and happen during the time of your first deal for you to get a second deal. This may sound harsh, but that is the reality. A network, and/or studio, is banking on your success otherwise, it would not be a wise investment for them.

TYPES OF DEALS

Act 3

There are four types of deals for writers and/or producers:

1. Overall Deal
2. First-Look Deal
3. Blind Script Deal
4. If/Come Deal

OVERALL DEAL

This is a deal that a network or studio makes with a writer or non-writing producer so that the projects are exclusive to that network or studio. This means, whether you are a writer or a non-writing producer, every project you develop while in this deal belongs to this network or studio.

The upside of this type of deal is that you have a "home." The network or studio will pay all your overhead costs, including salaries for your employees (i.e., development executives and assistants) and is eager to get your show produced.

The downside is if the network decides to pass (decline) on your project for any reason, perhaps because your project is not right for their brand, you would not be able to shop it around to other networks.

However, you would be able to bring your project to one of that network's sister networks. For example, if your deal is with FBC (FOX), and they pass, you can bring it to one of their sister networks, like FX, but not to others, like CBS. If there is not a good fit at any of their sister networks, you would not be able to work on the project during the time you are in this deal.

Now let's say your deal is with a studio and you want to sell to a network that said they will buy your show only if *their* sister studio can co-produce. Your studio would have to make a deal with the sister network or you wouldn't be able to sell to that network.
It should be noted that if the studio you are with is attached to a network, e.g., ABC Studios is attached to ABC, generally you

would *not* have to be exclusive to that network. You could sell your project to any network as long as a deal can be made by your studio with the other network. Keep in mind there are a few studios that only sell to the network(s) they are attached to. An example is CBS Productions.

The downside to having an overall deal with a studio is that you would be developing and producing shows exclusively for them. If they pass on one of your projects, you cannot shop it elsewhere.

An example of a writer/producer with studio overall deal is SHONDA RHIMES. For 12 years, she was in an overall deal with ABC Studios. All of her shows were/are on ABC, e.g., *Grey's Anatomy, How to Get Away with Murder*, and *Scandal*. They all fit ABC's brand. When she decided she wanted to branch out, she had to leave ABC. She subsequently made another overall deal with NETFLIX, where they brand to all audiences.

FIRST-LOOK DEAL

This is a deal that a network or studio makes with a writer or non-writing producer so they can get a "first look" at their projects. However, they are not exclusive to them.

This type of deal, like an Overall Deal, usually covers expenses for the writer or non-writing producer, i.e., a salary, an assistant, an office, etc.

The upside of a first-look deal with a network is that you have the freedom to sell your project to any other network after they pass on it. Networks pass on shows for a variety of reasons. One is that the show isn't working for them creatively so, even if they pass on it, and it works on another network, they don't take it too hard.

If you have a first-look deal with a studio, you also have the freedom to sell your project to another studio after they pass on it. However, most studios will support producers and their projects and not pass on them. If they did, they would be taking a big risk that another studio would snatch it up. What if it becomes a huge hit? It would be a terrible financial loss for them.

An example of this is what happened with the first *CSI* show. ABC Studios passed on the project, and ATLANTIS/ALLIANCE picked it up. This show has made billions of dollars for ATLANTIS/ALLIANCE, and ABC Studios made a HUGE mistake passing on it.

BLIND SCRIPT DEAL

This is a deal where a network or a studio hires a writer to write a TBD (to be determined) script. This type of deal is not one that a non-writing producer would ever get. This is solely for a writer. This deal happens when a network or a studio wants to be in business with a particular writer before that writer has pitched any ideas to them. This is for a writer who has made at least one successful TV show, movie, short, etc. A writer who has not had something produced would not be offered this type of deal.

IF/COME DEAL

This is a deal for a writer where they do not get paid upfront. The studio makes this deal because they would like to develop a project with a writer and take it out to the networks. "If" it sells, then the money "comes" and they get paid.

STRATEGIES FOR SELLING A TV SHOW

1. HOW TO GET STARTED

When I began working in television development in the 1990s (*discussed in the "Teaser" of this book*), the usual path writers/creators would take in order to sell their TV show or series was to work their way up the ranks in television production. Almost every writer had to start out on a TV show as an assistant and work their way up to becoming an executive producer. At that point, the networks might be open to their ideas for development.

Writers would then pitch their ideas to a studio or production company development executive. If they liked the idea, they would work together on the pitch. Then, they would bring the fleshed out pitch to the networks and hope for a bidding war from the Big Six.

This method still exists today. However, in the last few years there have been many examples of young writers who were able to by-pass this system. Today, a novice writer/creator can make a show and not have to sell it to a network! ANYONE with a phone, lap-top, the internet and a dream can make a TV show and, as dis-cussed, there are platforms for viewers to watch it, i.e., YouTube, and even new websites like SeedandSpark.com. This is also a way for young writers and producers to get noticed by networks and possibly SELL their show and ideas to them. It's not something that happens often, but today this is possible. This was impossible just 10 years ago.

Similarly, if you're looking to get noticed as a writer, and possibly work on a show, there are online contests, websites and consul-tants that can help get your script seen by producers and studio executives.

2. "WHO'S IN THE PACKAGE?"

You may hear this question from network executives when pitch-ing your project. If you are a non-writing producer or develop-ment executive at a studio describing your project to a network, they will want to know the auspices, or attachments, involved. This includes all the people and organizations affiliated in any way to the project. For the networks, it really is all about the whole package. They believe that knowing the team behind the project will give them a better idea of the project's potential.
Attaching key people to your project can definitely improve your chances of selling it. In fact, it is very desirable and sometimes

essential.   For young producers especially, it's better to have someone with known credits attached to your project.   "Key" is the important word here because there are some people you can attach that you may think any network would love to work with only to find they are not loved everywhere for every project.   By attaching these individuals, you may inadvertently hurt your project.   For this reason, it is important to learn everything you can about the network and/or studio that you want for your project.

There are some well-known individuals who are so beloved everywhere (at all networks) that they can get almost ANY project 'green-lit'.   This is usually because they have had a lifetime, or at least a good amount, of successful movies and/or TV shows.   It's important to note that these people are nearly impossible to attach.   They are few and far between.   But, if you are lucky enough to have a personal connection with them, or be discovered from your work, that would be wonderful.   This was the case with LENA DUNHAM who was discovered by JUDD APATOW.   They went on to make HBO's *Girls*.

This type of package should not be confused with another type of package called, an 'Agency Package.'   Here are the differences:

AGENCY PACKAGE

In the past, talent agencies, like Creative Artists Agency (CAA), William Morris Endeavor (WME) and United Talent Agency (UTA), got a package fee on shows when they represented key people or companies attached to a project.   Key people can be the creator/writer, non-writing producer, director, and/or star.

However, in April 2018, the WGA began the process of changing the way 'packaging' has been handled since the 1970's.   They believed practice of collecting package fees by agencies represents a conflict of interest to their clients (writers, producers, talent).   The reason they are looking into this now is because, over the years, agencies have started to act more like production companies, with a few actually having production companies within their organization.

Agencies are called, "Agency as Employer," and the Guild feels that certain agencies, i.e., WME and CAA, should not be active in the production, financing and distribution of shows. The agencies say they can do this because they have "related production entities," e.g., Endeavor Content, IMG Productions, Media Res and Bloom. CAA has Tornado Productions and Platform One.

The WGA believes that when these agencies got fees from the budgets of shows, it became more financially advantageous than getting commissions from individual clients. Therefore, it was not surprising that they were spending more time and effort into putting these packages together instead of getting their clients jobs. For the writers, it would be like having their employer also be their representative!

In 2016-2017, the WGA found that about 90 percent of the 300 shows produced that year were packaged! The Guild is in the process of revising the 42-year old "Artists' Manager Basic Agreement" (AMBA) with the Association of Talent Agents because of this huge conflict of interest on the part of agencies. They say the current agreement no longer serves their clients and at the time of this publication they have not come to a new agreement (11/2019).

The Guild believes that the talent agents have a fiduciary obligation to put the interests of their clients ahead of their own. The WGA members voted to terminate the old agreement and some 8 thousand writers have fired their agents. However, they are still able to work with managers and have their lawyers negotiate any jobs/deals.

This is a game-changer for independent producers and writers. The WGA has set up a new portal for producers to contact writers directly about open assignments and development (*Directories.wga.org*).

Act 3

ATTACHMENTS

The best and easiest way to get attachments is if you know, or are related to, someone you would like to attach to your project. Of course, this is not the case for most people.

The next best way is to network and reach out. In today's world, we are all much more accessible than we ever were. Almost everyone in the business has some sort of social media platform, including writers and executive producers. Reach out. If you get no response you are no worse off than if you hadn't tried.

As mentioned earlier, there are also websites connecting writers to producers (e.g., Inktip.com, Blcklst.com, VirtualPitchFest.com), as well as crowd-funding/funding websites (e.g., Slated.com, SeedandSpark.com).

The key is to NEVER GIVE UP!

3. DETERMINE IF YOU NEED A STUDIO

If you have a project that is really right for a particular network, going to their sister studio first and trying to get them on board would probably help the project.

However, today some writers and non-writing producers are able to go directly to the networks without having the support of a studio and/or production company. There are even certain networks that would prefer this because they then can "lay off" (give) the project to their own studio, which is financially beneficial for them.

If you do not fall into that category, having the support of a studio can be very beneficial for your project. The way to get a studio attached is:

a. Have your agent or manager help set up meetings.

b. If you are a producer without representation but have the rights to an IP, you can cold call studios to see if they will meet with you because you have this property.

c. If you have a showrunner attached, his/her representative will have definite opinions about attaching a studio.

Having a studio attached before you go out with your project is not always the best choice, so it's important to figure out if it will help yours move forward.

4. DETERMINE THE BEST FIT FOR YOUR SHOW

As discussed earlier, a network's brand is specific to their demographics. Do they cater to children, teens, the 18 to 49 year old demographics or the Baby Boomer generation? Do they produce science fiction dramas or historical series? Do they only produce reality series? Knowing the kind of programming that is working for each network will help you figure out where to go.

Some producers, studios and development executives feel you should also go to the networks that are not a seemingly good fit for your show or in line with their brand. I am one of those people because you never know. Sometimes networks are having conversations about wanting shows that are against their brand and it is possible that they are looking for exactly what you are selling. Give your project every chance. Even if you don't get the deal, you've gotten another chance to practice your pitch!

5. ARE YOU SELLING A SPEC SCRIPT?

Something that has just starting happening over the last five to ten years is for writers to write a spec script, and/or episodes, and/or bible of the series and submit it directly to the networks.

Writing a spec is a much more risky strategy than going out with a pitch. It requires the writer to do a lot of writing without the guarantee of getting paid. At one point, the market became so saturated with specs that the networks got less interested and excited about them. But the fact is that the writer/creator has total creative freedom with writing a spec. If the network read and liked your script, a meeting would be set up with the network to discuss the full series vision. Many shows have been sold this way, for example, *House of Cards, Desperate Housewives, Breaking Bad*.

When you are ready to send it out, there are two basic strategies.

1. Send the spec script to the network. If they like it, you can then meet with them to pitch the series.

2. Meet with the network first, and then leave the pilot script behind.

In my experience, I find the first strategy is better because if the network ends up not liking your script, you've wasted your time and theirs. It is best to come in after they like it and are already interested.

6. SHOULD YOU CHANGE ELEMENTS OF YOUR SHOW TO SELL TO A SPECIFIC NETWORK?

No. As discussed in previous chapters, when you are developing an idea and/or script, it is important to determine what the show is organically (its essence), and then figure out where it belongs.

Yes. You need to make sure your show is sellable (unless you are planning to finance it yourself).

The ideal scenario for pitching is to have many channels and outlets where you can sell your show. The more you have, the better your chances to sell it. Sounds logical, right?

The irony is that, even though there are over 50 places actively buying content today, writers usually find only about five places to pitch. All the networks have a very specific brand or niche.

The reality is that only one or two of them will be your show's "perfect" place.

7. TIMING IS EVERYTHING

Everything in life is about timing, and this is especially true when it comes to TV Development.

You may have heard the term "cult hit." This is when an excellent show does not find a big audience, but has found a niche and has developed its own fan base. This is an example of how timing is important in television. These cult hits have become hits because they got popular after they were released (usually with a specific demographic). If they were successful when they were released, then they would be *true* hits. They are successful all because of timing. It is said that these cult hit shows are ahead of their time.

Another example of good or bad timing: A show that works in 2001 may not be right for 2018, and vice versa. So if your show doesn't sell today, hold onto it. In time, the network and the world may be ready for it.

Similarly, as discussed earlier, understanding when to take your project out, and to which network, can make or break your success.

When taking out a PITCH:

- Make sure your pitch is ready. (*See Act 2 "The Pitch"*)

- Figure out which network to go to first, second, and so on. It is essential because you will learn how to improve your pitch each time. You do this by setting up your first pitch meeting where you think you have the *least likely* chance of selling your project. After that go to the network where you think is your *best* chance, the place that feels like the best fit.

- Have you gotten the attachments you wanted? The people

you have attached may have agents/managers/lawyers that will call for you as well.

- Visual Aids. Did you decide if your project needs them, and are they done?

8. DETERMINE IF YOUR PROJECT IS READY

How do you know when to take your project out to the market?

The answer is when it's ready.

Remember, there are no guarantees on selling it. You can only try. No one can tell you that you will sell your show for sure. If they do, they are selling you snake oil. The truth is, the world is changing, this business is changing and, if you keep working, doing what you love, using the tools in this book, you will have the best chances for success.

WHAT IS A TRANSMEDIA CAMPAIGN?

This is a strategy that consists of having a single narrative (story) that continues on through different mediums, e.g., web + twitter + TV.

At one end of the spectrum is a strict adaptation; that is translating from one medium into another. This would be a book that becomes a film, or a comic book that becomes a video game (e.g., film + comic book + video game).

At the other end of the spectrum is pure transmedia; where one medium "connects" with another. This happens when a book ends at the moment the film begins, or a comic book shows the origin of a hero that is featured in a video game.

Here are some examples of Transmedia projects:

- *Star Wars* – Perhaps the most extensive world that is built across platforms.
- *Star Trek*
- *The Matrix*
- *The Blair Witch Project* - Their online marketing campaign marks the first use of web storytelling.
- *Avatar*
- *Lost*

Much of Disney's programming for the youth market incorporates a transmedia campaign.

Many comic books have been adapted into video games, feature films, TV shows and animated shorts, e.g., *Superman* and *Spiderman*. This includes prequels, origin stories, sequels and spin-offs.

Having this strategy prior to selling your show can prove to be helpful. Oftentimes, when you achieve success in one medium, it seeds success in others.

WHAT IS A 'COMPETITIVE DEVELOPMENT REPORT'?

This is a list of projects the networks are actively buying for development. It's a good idea to start putting together this list because it will give you a sense of what each network is actually buying.

You can do this by reading the entertainment trade publications, e.g., Hollywood Reporter, Variety, and Deadline. When a network buys a pitch, there is usually an article about the people involved and the premise.

Each year, this is one of the jobs that a younger, lower-level executive would be responsible for putting together.

The Report consists of:

- The buyers
- Names of the projects they have in development
- Auspices (the people and affiliations attached)
- Logline or summary of the idea

Agents, managers, executives and producers feel it is imperative to have this list because, when selling shows, knowing what the networks have bought will inform them for both active and future development.

> *Side note: Each year, I find it interesting to try and guess which shows in the competitive development report will get picked up and have a pilot shot based solely on the logline and auspices. (This is only possible with broadcast networks as the cable networks don't usually just shoot pilots.) I read the scripts and watch the shot pilots. Then, I like to guess which pilots will be picked up to series.*

INDIE TV

Truly independent television (Indie TV) is when you get independent financing for a pilot and/or a season of a show to produce and sell it to the broadcasters. While independent financing does occur in the movie industry, in TV this is not the norm.

A good example in the feature (movie) business is Blumhouse Productions. The model is to have a really low-budget idea for a movie with no big stars attached. The goal is to make A LOT more money that it costs to produce. Great model! Sometimes a big star/talent will be a part of these low-budget movies, oftentimes taking a reduced acting rate while participating on the backend. That means after the film is released, if it is successful, they get a piece of the profits.

For TV it is different. Indie TV is far more expensive to produce than Indie movies. Currently, low-budget shows have not yet performed well or competed with the very expensive shows on TV. Typical budgets for shows are upwards of $4,000,000 an episode!

Also, the networks rarely buy fully-produced seasons of TV shows. In my career, I only know of a handful of successful shows that were independently produced and sold. A couple of examples are, *Always Sunny in Philadelphia* on Comedy Central and *High Maintenance* on HBO. One reason this is rare could be because the networks like to put their "stamp" on the show, meaning they like to have a say about the development of the show. By giving them a completed series, it takes them out of the creative process.

As previously stated, one way to make an Indie TV show on a very low budget that's available to everyone, is to air it on YouTube. This is where viewers can watch episodes of shows that were produced with money from investors and/or advertisers of that channel. These shows have yet to become mainstream and don't have the success model of the movie business, but that doesn't mean it won't happen. It just hasn't happened yet.

*****

Act 3

Assignments

Put together a Competitive Development Report by tracking projects in the trade publications. Then, take a guess as to which projects from the Report will become a pilot and/or series. (Of course, only for the ones that don't have series commitments.)

In six months or so, you can find out if you were correct. It's a good way to see if your instincts are right about which ideas will make a good series or not.

Another version of this assignment depends on whether or not you can get your hands on the scripts. If you are working as an assistant for someone in an agency, network or studio, or you know someone who is, perhaps you can get a copy of the scripts. Then you can read them and make an educated guess as to which ones will become great shows.

Yet another version of this assignment is being able to see the produced pilots before they air and then making your choices. If you are working as an assistant in the business, this is not difficult to get. If you don't, maybe you know someone who is. Ask around, sometimes they are even online.

These assignments are good exercises as they will help you when you are listening to, and pitching, ideas. You will know what works and doesn't work. The more knowledge you have of the current TV landscape, the more persuasive you can be when you are selling your show.

It is true that sometimes a great show does not become a hit, but some of them do become cult classics. This is due to timing as most are/were ahead of their time.

*****

ACT FOUR

Q & A with Industry Professionals

- Network Executives
- Studio Executives
- Production Company Executives
- Managers
- Agents

INTERVIEW WITH TED GOLD

Executive Vice President, Paramount Network (fka Spike)
Executive Producer, Parkes/MacDonald
Senior Vice President, FOX Network
Vice President, Spelling Entertainment

I met TED GOLD when we were both working at Spelling Entertainment. He is an accomplished, thoughtful, smart professional with a great sense of humor. He has always been very passionate about developing TV shows and I learned a lot from him. Ted went on to become a buyer at two different networks, and here's what he had to say about development. We met at the Viacom Hollywood offices in January, 2018.

Stephanie (SV): How did you get your start in TV Development?

Ted (TG): I sent out 70 resumes blind, around town. Eventually I got a call from STEPHEN J. CANNELL Productions. They were one of the last independent television suppliers and I got a job there as a messenger. Then, I was the receptionist and I soon learned about this area called, "Development." I volunteered to read scripts for them for free and give my comments. Then eventually I got a job as an assistant in the development department.

SV: Why did you choose development as opposed to a different job within the industry?

TG: I was an English major and I knew I wanted to work with writers. I realized quickly that this was the creative side of the business to making stories, making projects happen, and knew this is where I wanted to be. Thought it would suit my tastes, my skills.

SV: For people wanting to pursue a career in TV Development, what would you suggest they do?

TG: Read and watch as much material as you can! I would recommend writing coverage and develop your point of view on things. The most important thing is to understand what you like and why you like it. It's a lifetime endeavor. It changes over your life. But the more that you can analyze and express yourself, the better you get at it and, at the end of the day, that's what someone is going to hire you for. They are going to hire you for your tastes and your knowledge of writers and material.

SV: Regarding development, what would you do if you heard two very similar ideas, but the one you liked better came from a lesser known entity?

TG: That's a very good question. First of all, if there's a lot of overlap between the projects in terms of characters, I'd probably excuse myself from hearing one of them and let them know up front that I just heard this from another person. But forgetting the legality of it, I would go with the project I liked the best if I can. I would probably try to package it up. I mean, so much is about who is going to execute 50 episodes. So the lesser one might start off good, but it's harder to get on the air because nobody knows who that entity is. But I would probably lean towards the lesser one and see how I could bolster it and make it a sexier, stronger project by adding elements. Maybe you can combine the two.

SV: What is the most memorable pitch you've heard?

TG: (*laughing*) There are too many for me to answer, but one that comes to the top of my mind is when I was at Spelling (Entertainment), with you actually. It was a pitch that I developed which was the precursor pitch to *Lost*, which was developed with JEFFREY LIEBER, (creator/EP). It was a really well-thought-out, deep pitch because, at the time, it was almost considered a stupid idea to develop a show about people stuck on an island. Like, how could that last? And Jeffrey had a lot of specific ideas on how to keep that show going. That's one that comes to mind. I've heard, I think, over 1,000 pitches probably in my career. (*laughing*) I've got some funny ones, people falling asleep, people screaming, some pretty crazy ones.

SV: What is the most challenging aspect to developing a script?

TG: It's always different, but what I would have to say is figuring out what the story is. What is the core story and character point of view from which you are going to tell the story? I would always come back to that. What is the story or stories that you want to tell with your show? We can talk about the process. Sometimes it's working with writers and figuring out the best way to bring out the best in them. How do they respond to notes? Not just critique, but what's the best way to get them inspired and bring out their vision.

SV: What are your thoughts on spec scripts?

TG: Love 'em. I love spec scripts. I always try to read a spec script with an open mind. Still to this day I know how much work has gone into it and I think a good show can come from anywhere. Again, if it's a spec script without any track record, you have a giant hurdle of how do you get it on, and that would be a lot of producing.

SV: Which project that you produced are you most proud of?

TG: Well, I haven't produced a lot of projects. but I would say if I can count the one that is about to air right now, it's *Waco*.

SV: What about projects you developed?

TG: I really liked this project that was ahead of it's time that I developed at Spelling (Entertainment) called, *Kingpin*, which you probably remember. That was always one of my favorites. At

FOX, it was *Prison Break*. And people don't think it was a sexy show, but *Bones* was a very successful series.

SV: What is your favorite part of the TV Development process?

TG: I like research a lot. I like reading articles and books on a certain character or certain world. I can sometimes go down a rabbit hole doing research. I really enjoy doing that. I love figuring out who the characters are and breaking the story. That's probably number one. When it goes right, it really comes together and selling a project is fun. That's a pretty good feeling. Validation. All your hard-earned efforts... somebody thinks there is some merit.

SV: What do you feel is the biggest misconception about TV Development?

TG: The prolonged nature of it. That a project doesn't stop with development. That a project is not just about developing a script, it's about developing a team of people that can keep it going and keep developing it.

SV: What advice do you have for a young writers/creator who is looking to pitch a TV show?

TG: My advice would be to not spend too much time on a pitch when you are starting out. My advice would be to write your script. The reason is that there are too many people out there selling shows. You're competing against a lot of big name people.

SV: What do you feel will be different about the process of TV Development, specifically in five years or ten years?

TG: Things are much more package-dependent now. If you want to compete, there is so much out there. How do you get people to notice? One of the ways is having great people on your project, working on your project and in your project. That seems like a trend that is going to continue. Also, I don't know if this will happen in five years, but this format of half-hour vs. hour vs. two-hour movies… it all goes out the window. Maybe we can make a 43-minute project? Maybe we can make a 12-minute project? I think the formats of the projects should be more driven by the projects themselves vs. trying to fit a round peg into a square hole. I think some of that is changing now.

SV: What about Indie Television?

TG: The bottom line is, if you're talking about traditional scripted television with actors, it's a lot of money to figure out how to finance it. I do think there will be people who will figure it out. It seems that to me with the old model, with advertising content, seems to be diminished. Ratings are all down. Nobody knows how they are going to make money. Still, the advertisers need to find ways to get their product out there. So where are they going to go? Maybe there will be people who will pull in a few advertisers to sponsor their own projects independently.

SV: In today's market, what is the measure of a successful show?

TG: Depends who you are, depends what your job is (*laughing*).

SV: As a network executive?

TG: I am mostly concerned of how my project is viewed creatively, as a project of quality and as a project that would fit the brand, both internally and externally. So I would say reviews. Internally if a lot of people are really excited about our project and then, if that gets reaffirmed on the outside that people like our projects.

At the end of the day, even though I can't control it, if you don't get ratings, you're out. So ratings are super important. You're still judged by the thing that is much harder to measure - ratings. But ratings themselves are changing. It used to be live plus same day, now it's live plus three.

Side note: 'Live plus three' refers to the ratings during a live show plus the next three airings of the show.

SV: Do you think everyone is going to be streaming, and that traditional broadcast and cable TV will go away in some way?

TG: Yes, I think it will go away in some way. But I've been saying that for ten years. So it's slow. It's always slower than I think it's going to be. I mean, who wants to watch a program live anymore? Who wants to rush home at 8 o'clock on a Thursday night to watch something? Very few people, unless it's news or sports. People don't really care. So it's all going to be on-demand and streaming, if you ask me. I don't know if all the channels will disappear or the linear channels will disappear. It might become some kind of hybrid, which is kind of what you're seeing now where if you miss something that is live, you can find it somewhere streaming, although it takes forever to figure out where. And then what is TV? Most kids don't even watch a lot of TV, which is a whole bigger question.

*****

INTERVIEW WITH ANDREW PLOTKIN

Senior Vice President, Drama Development, Sony
Head of Development, New Regency
Senior Vice President, SYFY
Vice President, Drama Development, Warner Brothers

ANDREW PLOTKIN was the Warner Brothers development executive I worked with when I worked for JERRY BRUCKHEIMER. He is professional, charismatic and fun. When his boss at Warner Brothers left to start his own production company, he asked Andrew to join him, which he did. He has worked on all sides of the TV Development business and still loves it. He's currently a development executive at Sony. We met on the Sony lot in February, 2018.

Stephanie (SV): How did you get your start in the TV business?

Andrew Plotkin (AP): My first job was working at a studio. Do you remember Rysher Entertainment?

SV: I do.

AP: I was an intern there for maybe five months or so and a desk opened up, and I became an assistant to the head of the television department. I did that for about a year. I got promoted off that desk and was off and running.

SV: Is that where you learned about TV Development?

AP: Yes, that's exactly how. I realized this is a thing, a business, a career.

SV: Why did you choose to do TV Development as opposed to doing something else in the business?

AP: Originally I thought I was going to be on the movie side of the business, but I soon learned about the pace of TV and realized I don't have the patience to work on the movie side. I saw that, with TV, you have to constantly feed the beast.

SV: So were you promoted at Rysher to an executive pretty fast and not an assistant very long?

AP: Yeah, Rysher had a lot of shows. It was good timing. I got lucky.

SV: You've been a producer, a writer, a studio and a network executive. What was your favorite role and why?

AP: If I had to choose one as a favorite I would choose producer because you are constantly learning. No one project is ever the same. They all bring their own sets of obstacles and you have to learn how to overcome them. It was just the most kind of rapid growth as a producer. I mean, I do the same thing now but, as a producer, you are more hands-on. You go from the script to the budget to marketing. You touch every part of the process in a more meaningful way. A studio executive is less detailed-oriented and has more of an overview, and the volume is just SO much more in this job.

SV: Does your role at SONY today differ from when you were a studio executive at Warner Bros. 15 years ago?

AP: In terms of the job, not so much. The job's the job. It's more or less the same. What's different is the business, like at Warner's it was relatively easy to sell a show. They (the networks) were like, "Yeah, we'll buy it." They (the networks) would take 'flyers' on things, whereas now good is not good enough. It's got to be rock solid. The package is very important. Today it's more about how we put it together, the sales and packaging.

SV: You pursued becoming a writer at one point in your career. Why did you decide not to pursue that anymore?

AP: It was too lonely. When I was in my pajamas at 3:30 in the afternoon and I hadn't left the house, I realized it wasn't for me. I needed more immediate feedback. Like I was saying before, I get so impatient. I love being really, really busy bouncing from one task to the other. As a writer, the pace is like way different, way slower. I love writing, but I couldn't do it every day. It has to be the only thing in the world you can possibly see yourself doing.

SV: What can a writer or producer just starting out do to get their projects in front of you?

AP: As a writer, it can't be unsolicited for legal reasons. It has to come through an agent or lawyer. As a producer, be an aggressive producer. Pick up the phone and say, "I have a great idea." Be persistent and keep at it. Tell the assistants.

SV: What kinds of shows do you like to develop?

AP: For me, it's all about character and emotion. Whatever the show is, it all starts with character. Whether it's a pure soap opera, or a genre high-concept *Game of Thrones* kind of thing, it doesn't matter. I love all of it as long as the character stuff is very, very powerful. I think that's the only reason why TV works.

SV: What is the most memorable pitch you've heard?

AP: I think the most memorable pitch to this day was at Warner's and it was with SHAUN CASSIDY. He had gotten the rights and access to the ELTON JOHN library of songs so he created a show using characters from his songs. He created this whole mythology using some of his really well-known songs. We were pitching it to GAIL BERMAN at FOX, and he's pitching it just regular, and then he gets up and it's SHAUN CASSIDY, and he can sing! So he starts singing, performing in the room and we're just like, "What's going on here? This is amazing." So that was pretty cool.

SV: Did they buy it?

AP: They did NOT buy it. I think it was ahead of its time. They didn't know what to do with it.

SV: So it never got made? You didn't sell it?

AP: No.

SV: Would you pursue it today?

AP: Yeah, in a heartbeat.

SV: What is the best script you developed that didn't get made, and what happened?

AP: (*laughing*) Oh, my God, there's like a million of them. Okay, so one of my favorites, I think LIONSGATE is doing it right now actually. It's a book series called, "The Kingkiller Chronicle." It's a grounded, fantasy, period-piece, like *Game of Thrones*, and it's an amazing story. It's basically the *Batman* story. It's about this kid who sees his parents and his whole extended family get murdered by these essentially immortal, supernatural, bad guys. So he devotes his life to train himself to ultimately confront these really bad people, kill them and get revenge. But underneath it all, it had this incredible musical element. It's one of the best book series I've ever read in my whole life. I mean the script was amazing. We sold it to NBC and it should have been a cable show. They kind of tried to water it down, give it a franchise essentially, and it just didn't work. That was disappointing.

SV: Now, you said LIONSGATE is doing it.

AP: Yeah, I think when the rights lapsed they picked it up. I think they are double-developing it as a movie and a series.

SV: *Probably for cable?*

AP: For sure. It has to be on cable.

SV: *What would you say is the most challenging aspect to developing a script?*

AP: I think the most challenging aspect is making it emotionally resonate. The challenge is that the writer may be hearing it and seeing it one way that can feel incredibly emotional, but if it's not translating to the page you're at a major impasse. So how do you get from inside somebody's head to the page? It's very hard. That's tough.

SV: *What is your favorite part of the TV Development process?*

AP: My favorite part is getting that first draft and seeing if there's anything there. Is there a there, there, and then honing it from there. That's the best.

SV: *What's the most challenging part of your job?*

AP: For me, the challenging part of my job is pitching it because you only have about twenty minutes to communicate a lot of information and to get the people (the network) to feel what it is you're talking about. They hear like fifty pitches a day, or whatever it is, so they are way ahead of you. They know what the show is the second you sit down. So how do you get them (the network) to care about it? And that's tough.

SV: *What is your most successful project you are proud of?*

AP: I was very proud of this show called, *Being Human*, when I was at the SYFY network because, at the time, the network was saying they wanted to elevate their programming and do something not cheesy. It ended up being satisfying on a few levels. One, it was a format that we got from the UK and we were having a hard time finding a writer that could do the character stuff and the genre stuff. It was about a ghost and a werewolf and a vampire who live together. But it was a real drama, so I decided to put these two writers together. It turns out they were married, but they were not a writing team at that time. Together they made the perfect, in theory, writer [for this project] and it worked out. They went on to create a very grounded, emotional and intense monster movie, basically. It was really cool.

SV: What advice do you have for writers, creators, and producers looking to sell a show?

AP: I would say the first two questions to ask yourselves are, "Why is whatever it is you're doing relevant now?" and "Why should anyone care about it?" You gotta remember, there are so many choices. That's what I ask myself, "Why now?" and "Why do I care about whatever the series is saying?"

SV: Being that SONY is an independent studio, meaning they are not aligned with any network, what are your thoughts about the future of Indie studios?

AP: We are lucky because we can truly work with pretty much anybody out there. We are very entrepreneurial. I think that to remain an Indie you have to be more and more entrepreneurial and figure out creative ways to get stuff done. We're thinking a lot right now, for example, about starting to sell a show internationally and then maybe bringing it back here. So, I think that's the key. You have to constantly change up the game and figure out ways that you kind of slip through the cracks and find a niche. Everything is changing so fast you have to be ahead of those changes.

SV: Do you think one day they (indie studios) will go away and networks will only work with their in-house studio?

AP: No, I think that that is cyclical. I think they (the networks) go through phases of, "We're only going in-house," and then they realize that it's not the best way to get the best creative material.

SV: Is there an Indie TV model similar to Indie movies?

AP: Not as successful because that movie model is driven by the financing. When you're selling here, people don't need your money. It's nice to presell something and go to NBC and say you can have this at a fraction of the license fee. Maybe that works, but what you're giving up is the emotional investment of that show. If they love a show, they are going to keep it on the air and make it work. If it's more of a transactional kind of thing, they will feel they can cancel in a heartbeat and it doesn't matter.

SV: What is the measure of a successful show?

AP: A smaller, diehard, loyal fan base. That's how these shows on Netflix and cable come back. If they ever let us know what those numbers are, what the ratings are… However, they are probably not that big, but they are super-consistent and satisfying a key demographic.

SV: That's really for cable or streaming. What about broadcast?

AP: I guess for either. The true measure is being able to cut through all the clutter.

*****

INTERVIEW WITH CHRISTINA DAVIS

Partner, Maniac Productions
SVP, Drama Development, CBS

I met CHRISTINA DAVIS when she was an assistant at CBS and I was an assistant at Spelling Entertainment. Over the years, both of us have worked on many of the same TV shows. Christina rose through the ranks at CBS and, in recent years, I have been pitching to her as an independent producer.

*She recently left the network and partnered with writer/producer, MICHAEL SEITZMAN to form Maniac Productions. They have an overall deal with Disney (ABC Studios). When I met with her, they had a show in post-production for FREEFORM called, **Cleopatra,** and have a pilot that was picked up at ABC called, **Staties**. Here is an excerpt from my interview with her in January, 2018.*

Stephanie (SV): When did you find out what Television Development is?

Christina (CD): My first job out of college was a receptionist job at TV Guide. I worked in advertising for less than a year, and one of the editorial writers made the jump over to a show called, *Sisters*, with SELA WARD, on the Warner Brothers lot. She came back to visit one day and asked me what I wanted to do. I told her I was in job transition and I didn't want to continue working in advertising. She called me that night and asked if I could come and be the writers' assistant for this show, which was in its sixth year. So I got a little bit of a handle of what TV Development was there. But when that show was cancelled, I went into the Warner Bros. lot temp pool and I got a call one morning that there is a job in de velopment. NINA TASSLER (former development executive and CBS chairman), needed a temp. I didn't know what development was but, the minute she zipped in and sat down and started making her calls, I started to piece together that there is a studio executive who is the liaison between the writers, directors and the network. That was it! I was in hook, line and sinker! And I fell in love with her too!

SV: Why did you choose working in TV Development as opposed to a different job within the industry?

CD: While working for Nina, I learned that there is somebody that has a year-round job that sells to the network, and there is a network development person that has a year-round job that buys from the studios. That appealed to me because, as a writer's assistant, I felt the instability of the business. I thought maybe I wanted to be a writer but, once I met Nina and I learned what development was and the stability of that and the creativity was still there, I realized it was a better fit for my personality. It involved building relationships with writers. You have a lot of volume.

That's the other thing I liked, being busy all the time. From the studio, it's selling, producing pilots... You're in the trenches with the writers. It also blends nicely with my need for structure and stability, but it leans directly into a creative role which has been rewarding and fulfilling for the last 22 years. It was the perfect job for me!

SV: For people wanting to pursue a career in TV Development, what would you suggest they do?

CD: My suggestion is if you're right out of college and you don't have a job lined up, which most people don't, I would say if you are a writer, or if you want to be in development, go to an agency. That is going to be the biggest education of the business, which is changing so much. I would say spend a year there, get your hands dirty and learn everything that you can. Listen in on those calls, talk to clients about the industry and then pursue what you want to do. If you're a writer, keep writing. If you want to be a development executive you need to know what the state of the business is and who's who. Try to get into a studio, a pod (production company), someone that's doing what you want to do and learn from them.

SV: What kinds of shows do you like to develop?

CD: Well, I've been at CBS for 20 years so my target has been very narrow. There are exceptions, but my focus has been character-driven, closed-ended, story-telling. In my new role as a producer, I am excited to expand upon this experience and add more serialized dramas to my development slate. Currently, we are developing *Cleopatra*, which will be a very different kind of show than I've developed in the past.

SV: Regarding development, what would you do if you heard two very similar ideas, but the one you liked better came from a lesser known entity?

CD: For me, it is about the idea. I can always package and add elements in order to help the writer, but the most important element for me is the idea.

SV: What is the most memorable pitch you've heard?

CD: *The Good Wife.* It was timely. It was political. It was from the point of view of the woman standing next to the man being accused. She had to rebuild her life as a lawyer. It was a legal thriller. It was all these things. I loved it and I remember it like it was yesterday.

SV: What is the best script you've developed that didn't get made? What happened?

CD: *The Rainmaker*, based on JOHN GRISHAM'S novel. I developed this show while at CBS with my now current producing partner, MICHAEL SEITZMAN. I loved it from the beginning and, for whatever reason, it didn't get picked up. But, because I love it so much and believe it deserves to get on the air, we are working on repackaging it now and it will hopefully be on the air someday.

SV: What is the most challenging aspect to developing a script?

CD: Seeing the vision of the writer end up on the page. It is so exciting to hear a great pitch and then you go through the story area, the outline and the script process. Then, if you get the script and it doesn't end up as good on the page, doesn't live up to the expectations from the pitch, it's unfortunate and probably the most challenging aspect of developing a script.

SV: What are your thoughts about spec scripts?

CD: I love spec scripts. I encourage all writers to always write original spec scripts, as opposed to specs of existing shows. Showrunners like to read original scripts vs. an example of their show because it showcases the writer's unique voice. MARC CHERRY (writer/creator/executive producer), really proved that and changed the business with his spec of *Desperate Housewives*. He pitched the idea around town and no one bought it, so he decided he needed to write it. He took a chance and it paid off. It rebranded ABC!

SV: What do you love, or what is your favorite part of the TV Development process?

CD: I love hearing a really great pitch and having it be realized to pilot and ultimately series!

SV: What are the most challenging part and least favorite part of your job?

CD: After working on a season of development with hearing upwards of 400 pitches, developing 50 scripts that become eight to ten pilots, and then going to New York for ten days where it is screened for the company, getting their opinions and then going to Las Vegas where the pilots are tested with the public, and getting their opinions... My development ends up getting dwindled down to maybe two to three shows getting picked up to series, and hopefully, with one to two of them staying on the air. The odds are staggering.

SV: What are your thoughts on Indie TV? Is there a successful Indie TV model that is similar to the Indie movie model?

CD: Not in broadcast television. It can exist and does outside of broadcast television, but I do not believe it would ever work in broadcast.

SV: What do you feel will be different about the process of TV Development, specifically in five years, ten years?

CD: I believe the process for broadcast television development will be changing because it has to. The current broadcast model does not work because it is still driven by advertisers. The ratings are dwindling and it has to change because it can no longer be about who is watching live TV. No one watches shows live anymore, with the exception of sports and news.

SV: In today's market, what is the measure of a successful show?

CD: Awards, accolades, being recognized by word of mouth. A perfect example is *Handmaid's Tale*. Because it has won awards, people will sign up for the "30-day free subscription" on Hulu and binge-watch the show. They will then see the other shows and probably become a subscriber. It's all about subscriptions.

*****

INTERVIEW WITH ADAM BONNETT

Executive Vice President, Original Programming, Disney Channel

I met ADAM BONNETT through one of my students at UCLA. His former assistant told him about my class and Adam offered to be a guest speaker. At that time, I had not developed any children's ("kid") shows. After his lecture that night, I was intrigued about the opportunities and benefits of that kind of programming and decided to pitch to him. My partners and I are currently working on several new ideas to bring to him. I met with him in his offices on the Disney lot in February, 2018.

Stephanie (SV): What was your first job in this business?

Adam (AB): I was an intern while still at NYU film school. I worked for GERALDO RIVERA and for CNN. Then my first job was working as an assistant at Nickelodeon.

SV: Did you know you ultimately wanted to work in children's programming?

AB: No, I did not. When I took the job at Nickelodeon, it was 1990. My favorite show was on MTV was Cindy Crawford's *House of Style*. It was about fashion, design and architecture and stuff like that. This was before HGTV and all the different DIY shows that are out there now. It was the only way to watch that kind of stuff, and I loved to watch it and wanted to work on that show. I thought if I take a job at Nickelodeon, which was in the same building as MTV, somehow I would make my way to working on that show, which was somewhat foolish because it was on a different network. But once I got into the groove at Nickelodeon, I realized how unstable and fickle the audience was for MTV and how loyal the kid audience was at Nickelodeon. Also I liked that, in terms of creating shows, it had a little bit more longevity and the whole concept of creating kid stars was really intriguing to me and certainly how merchandise can come out of content. That felt interesting and attractive to me. So then I made the choice to stick around in this kid's business and not try and go to the more glitzy, sexy division of Viacom like MTV or VH-1.

SV: What is the biggest difference in being a network executive today from when you started?

AB: When I was at Nickelodeon, my job at Disney today didn't really exist because the great thing about my job now is that I oversee series development, movie development, current series, casting/talent relations and short-form programming. The short-form division didn't even exist because we have these new platforms that need content. These are new businesses that never existed and being an executive who oversees series and movies is pretty unique. You don't see that all the time. Back when I was at Nickelodeon, they didn't even make movies.

Also, making sure that our talent grows up on our shows happy and healthy is so important to us and that's a priority that has evolved over the years. So it's my job that's really unique and it's always challenging me.

SV: What would you say are the main goals when developing programming for kids? ˙

AB: I think that you are targeting a very specific audience who's as young as six and as old as 11 to 14. That's the kids business. The preschool business is kids aged two to five. So whether you're developing for a preschooler or kids, you have to craft a show that speaks to a very specific audience. For me, I like the specificity of coming up with an idea for a kid that is as young as six and as old as eleven. They're going to love this concept or this character. Also, we're boxed in. We can't develop stuff that is political or about sex or even too much pop culture. We are trying to create stuff that is very "evergreen." I actually like having those guardrails. It forces us to be a little bit more inventive, clever. Then, on top of that, we are the Disney channel, so it's not just for kids, it's for Disney Kids. So you have to constantly keep "Big Disney" in mind and make sure that whatever we are making really feels part of that brand as well.

SV: Do pitches mainly come in to you or do you come up with the ideas internally?

AB: A lot of the areas we develop we do come up with internally, and then we go to writers and tell them we want to do a show about a girl who's a pop star that feels special, and what's the twist? They would come back to us with what turned out to be, *Hannah Montana.* That's not the only way. We went to TERRI MINSKY, who created *Andi Mack* and said, "What do you want to write?" She said, "I love mothers and daughters," and she came to us with a pitch about a mother and a daughter show but with a very unique mother and daughter relationship. It varies, but we tend to come up with the ideas ourselves. We have this movie called *Zombies* coming out in two weeks, and it was originally called *Zombies and Cheerleaders* because it's about the sort of lovable zombies and these antagonist cheerleaders. We came up with it because it has two sets of cliques that didn't belong together. We gave the title to the writers and said, "We want to do a show about zombies and cheerleaders, whatcha got?" And it's amazing what they came back with. With *Descendants,* we said we wanted to do a movie about the children of the Disney villains, "Come to us with characters," which is what they did.

SV: For people wanting to develop shows for kids, what do you suggest they do?

AB: The first thing you have to do is to remember what you loved as a kid and the kinds of content you would want to immerse yourself in...going back to your own childhood and getting excited about that time in your life. You also have to remember to look at things through a lens. You have to be able to say, "Yeah, I think this is funny, but would a kid think this is funny?" Remember to have a kid's point of view.

SV: What advice do you have for writers/creators looking to sell a TV show to you?

AB: The best thing is to write what is personal to you. You have to have a personal connection to what you write. If you are trying to sell something to Disney, and you don't have a personal connection, or it doesn't speak to any personal experience you had as a kid, it will be hard to sell.

If you don't have any credits as a writer, always attaching yourself to a person who does is a good thing. Also, every network has incredible fellowship programs that give opportunities to up-and-coming creators and writers. For us, we get to work with a lot the writers who are part of the ABC fellowship program. They get assigned to shows or ABC/Disney shows and that's a great opportunity. Then, if you prove yourself and they want to hire you as a writer, you're done.

Another way is to get a job on the network executive side. We have a writer on *Andi Mack* that started out as an assistant here. When the show went into production, he came to us and said, "I love that show you guys developed and I want to work on it." Because we had a relationship with him and trusted him, we were like, "We're going to give him this opportunity."

SV: What is the most memorable pitch you've heard?

AB: Well, we do get the crazies who dress up like a clown and come in with props. But, when I think about the most memorable pitch or casting meeting, I think about when the JONAS BROTHERS came in. At the time, they were just singers. They did a scene for us to show that they could act, but then JOE JONAS jumped on the table and started singing out the scene as a MICK JAGGER type of actor/dancer/singer preforming for us. I will never forget when he shocked us by jumping on the table in the middle of the conference room. Then recently there was a pitch where the writer was pitching a show about a family who lives with a robot and he hired an actor to come in as the robot in a robot suit. It was annoying and distracting. For a good pitch, you want to talk about the characters and stories, and these props often take away from the pitch.

SV: *Are you open to original spec scripts?*

AB: Definitely open as long as they are submitted the right way, through an agent or manager for legal reasons. Of course, it's hard to nail it on your own, but if you've already done it...

SV: *Have you bought any specs that have become a show?*

AB: I know we've done it on the movie side, for sure. As a series, no, not specs, but we've bought busted scripts from other networks.

SV: *What is your favorite part of the TV Development process?*

AB: Two parts. The first is when you hear the idea that feels where you say to yourself, "Why didn't I think of that?" It's just so good, like *Descendants* was. It was a great idea. The other part is when you sit in a casting session and the lead kid... you see it. You're like, "wow" that kid is not only the character we are trying to cast, but depending on the project, you have the sense that this kid is going to be a star when they grow up. If you look at our history, starting with HILLARY DUFF, RAVEN SIMONE, MILEY CYRUS, SELENA GOMEZ, DEMI LOVATO, DOVE CAMERON, the list goes on and on. We have a great track record and on the boys' side, ZACK EFRON, ROSS LYNCH, and THE JONAS BROTHERS. To be able to find talent at a young age, nurture it and see them go on to be such a big part of pop culture... and it means so much to kids and teenagers. It's really fulfilling.

SV: What is your most successful/proud project that you were a part of?

AB: Gosh, really good question. Different projects for different reasons. I think about *That's So Raven* as our first sitcom. I was so proud of starting the sitcom business for us back in the day because so much of what has defined the Disney Channel after that has been sitcoms. So to start that genre at the channel, which was like 16 years ago, was really exciting. It was also that RAVEN was the first African American girl to star in a sitcom with her name in the title. The only other show at the time was MOESHA, which was played by BRANDI, and she was playing a character vs. RAVEN, where we used her name in the title. She wasn't a conventional teenage girl. She was incredibly talented, unique in her own way. She had a different comedic point of view about the world. She felt vulnerable and special. I'm really proud of launching that show. I know it meant so much to kids back in the day, and now as millennials watch her again, but [this time] as a mom, is really fulfilling. Also, *Hannah Montana* because of the commercial appeal of the show and everybody remembers that show. I think that show really merged music and kids television story-telling in such a unique way. I used to oversee animation and I developed two shows that I'm really proud of. One is *The Proud Family*, the first animated series about an African American family. The creator really wanted to animate and create a show about his family, and for a show to feel so broad yet real was something that I was really proud of. Lastly, was this cartoon called, *Kim Possible, about a female crime-fighter and it just felt ahead of its time. You look at all the crime-fighter shows out today, there's nothing about a teenaged girl. To introduce a real action adventure show that still felt real, I felt was really ahead of its time.

> Side note: *About nine months after our meeting, Disney announced it was bringing back Kim Possible as a live-action movie. It's will be done and released in 2019. I didn't call Adam to see if our conversation had anything to do with this reboot, but I'd like to think it did!*

SV: In today's market, what would you say is the measure of a successful show?

AB: Any show where people are generally passionate about it. When a kid lights up when they talk about the show, when they want to stay home and see it live so they can talk about it the next morning, that's what gets me up in the morning. You don't see that a lot with adults. For us, what matters the most is that passion a kid has in how much they love the show. Then I love to see that passion reflected in other ways so it's not just, "I watched the show," it's "I want to dress up like the characters," or "I love the show so much I want to listen to all the songs from the show/ movie," or reading the fan mail from the kids because an actor or character means so much to them that they're going to take the time to write a letter. That's when you know you've got something special.

*****

INTERVIEW WITH TAYLOR LATHAM

President, Escape Artists Production Company
Development Executive, Double Feature

I sent a spec script to JASON BLUMENTHAL, one of the founders of Escape Artists, because my production team and I were looking for partners. TAYLOR LATHAM is the President of their TV division. I told her about this book. She graciously accepted my request for an interview and I met with her in their offices on the SONY lot in February, 2018.

Stephanie (SV): When did you find out what TV Development was?

Taylor (TL): I was working for MICHAEL SHAMBERG and STACEY SHER at their film production company, Double Feature, and I kept reading stuff that felt more like television than film, which I kept bringing to them and they finally said, "Oh yeah, let's get into television." So, I got into it organically. I was running both their television and film for them. After I had been there for six years, we got a first-look deal with AMC and developed our first show with them, *Into the Badlands*, which is still going strong.

SV: For people wanting to pursue a career in TV Development, what do you suggest they do?

TL: I say this to anyone who wants to work in the business at all, go work for a year at an agency. If you want to get in Television Development, try to get a job on a TV lit person's desk. It's like being a freshman in college. You will learn the people's names that matter. You will be exposed to a bunch of scripts, both good and bad. You will learn about the deal-making process. It's basically like year one of college. If you start out at a production company, as great and as warm as a production company can be, you will never have the volume. Also, there are so many people who are essentially your age starting out in the business at the same spot and with all the other assistants on that floor or in that department they kind of become your freshman year friends. I still know everyone I started off that first year with and we are all still good friends. Now they are top-level executives and agents, and I can pick up the phone to call them. I have better access to those people when I need information and that's invaluable.

SV: What can someone with no credits do to get their project in front of you?

TL: When you are at a company like this, it's kind of hard. For legal reasons, we need for it to come through a lawyer or an agent or a manager so that later on we are not sued. But, I say get your scripts read by as many people as possible. Submit them to every contest you can think of. Almost all winners, even the top ten, will get snatched up by managers. That's the best way to break into the business. Or, get an internship at a production company and walk into an executive's office and say, "Hey, I know I'm just an intern, but I have a great script."

SV: What kind of shows do you like to develop?

TL: I like all across the board. I love dramas. I think all dramas should have an element of soap opera to them. I think that's what keeps you coming back. Even if there's an underlying mystery, which I also think is a great vehicle, the sort of thing that keeps you coming back week-to-week is the soap opera between the characters. I think any time you can have a soap element in a show, that's what I look for.

SV: What is the most memorable pitch that you've gone out with?

TL: When AL GOUGH and MILES MILLAR came up with their pitch for *Into the Badlands*, even though it was hugely world-building, I could see it all. They had thought about the whole world down to the nitty-gritty. They really almost didn't leave anything up to my imagination with a central character who had a really interesting journey. The main character is an assassin who figures out he wants a better life and realizes he has to atone for all of his sins. You can understand how it's going to take him like five to seven seasons to reach enlightenment. But, within this world they created, there were so many different divisions and factions, and they each had names. It was just the world-building that they had such a handle on that you heard it and you were completely confident that they were going to create that world on the screen.

SV: Is it important for you to have projects come with attachments?

TL: No. I just need really good writing. I mean, that's what Escape Artists does. We're good at putting the package together.

SV: What is the best project you developed that didn't get picked up? And what happened?

TL: We shot a pilot called, *Prototype* for the SYFY network. The reason why Escape Artists fell in love with it was it was a very character-driven show and the sci-fi elements to the show were pretty minimal. The character development was in the forefront. What happened was SYFY bought it because it didn't have a lot of sci-fi elements to the show and, unfortunately, they passed on it because it didn't have a lot of sci-fi elements to the show,* so that was heart breaking.

> *Side note: *This is sometimes the irony with TV Development. A network will say they want one thing and then when you deliver that, they change their minds.*

Act 4

SV: What would you say is the most challenging aspect to developing a script?

TL: I would say getting the writer's vision to come through on the page, and sometimes it takes pulling teeth getting it out of them. A lot of times they have great, big, grand ideas, but focusing it on to the page is the challenge.

SV: What is your favorite part of the development process?

TL: I love getting into the weeds with writers in terms of big ideas and making sure the mythology of their big ideas or the architecture of the whole season is logically thought out. Obviously, it all starts with a great pilot script, but the pilot should be somewhat of a mini-microcosm of the whole series. If you can't really feel that you've got a handle of the architecture of the whole series from the pilot script, then you've got some work to do. That's the fun of it for me.

SV: What is your least favorite part of the process?

TL: *(laughing)* Selling. Even if three places want something and two places say no and one place says yes, you still can't help but feel the rejection of the places that said no.

SV: What are your thoughts on Indie television?

TL: The future is always changing but, at the moment, networks like to have their fingerprints on their stuff. So unless you want to upload it to YouTube, it's hard to get the financial backing. It's hard to get the executive investment in it when you want to deliver everything on a platter.

That's not to say that if you've got a bunch of friends who are good actors and a friend who can be a great cameraman not to go out and film an eight minute presentation that sometimes can incredibly help. But otherwise, at the moment, you're still stuck with putting it up on YouTube, or potentially some other sites. There are not a ton of those. It's possible. It's just harder.

SV: What do you feel will be different about the process of TV Development in five or ten years?

TL: It feels like the last few years have been very heavy on IP and, with more outlets opening up I feel it will become even more IP dependent. That's just my prediction. When you have a new company that is just getting off the ground and you are just trying to get eyeballs, they want it to be something big. There's a reason why Amazon bought the *The Lord of the Rings* IP. They had eyeballs already and even they were like, "What is gonna be our big, almost pre-sold idea?" I think that any sort of new companies popping up are gonna want those anchors.

SV: In today's market, what do you think is the measure of a successful series?

TL: That you get more than one season!

*****

INTERVIEW WITH GEOFF SILVERMAN

Partner, Cartel Entertainment
Literary Manager

I met GEOFF SILVERMAN at the William Morris Agency. We were assistants in the same department. He has gone on to become the co-founder of the production and management company, Cartel Entertainment. He has built an impressive list of clients. His offices in the heart of Hollywood are well-equipped with edit bays, a sound stage and an executive suite. Here's what he had to say during our meeting in February, 2018.

Stephanie (SV): How did you get your start in the business?

Geoff (GS): After graduating UCLA, I got a position as an assistant for the William Morris Agency working in the talent department for AMES CUSHING and JOAN HYLER. They had some pretty amazing, big, big clients. Working in the trenches.

SV: When did you know you wanted to be a manager?

GS: Pretty soon on I realized that, if I were a manager, I could produce. When I was working for BRETT RATNER, I started 'hip-pocketing' clients. The thing that I first saw, which was way, way ahead of the curve, was taking on diversity writers and really championing them. I had so many diversity clients who were not on staff. They were in writing programs and now they are up to Co-EP level. I have this guy, ANUPAM NIGAM, who is the co-executive producer on the new *Grey's Anatomy - Fire House* spin-off. When I found him, he literally was an NYU medical student. I have this guy, named ANGEL DEAN LOPEZ, who this past year was the number two on three shows. I have this guy, BRYAN OH. He was a staff writer on The *OC* when I signed him. He's now the Co-EP running the room on *Zoo* for APPELBAUM and NEMEC.

SV: Are you a producer on all of your clients' projects?

GS: Not always. I always put my client's interests first. If there's a project that I bring to the client like, "Here's a book or a piece of IP," and I feel comfortable to say to them, "Hey, Cartel is looking to be a producer," then we would remain involved, but my main focus is staffing. Until my clients get to the point where they are showrunners, it's really hard for me to attach myself and have Cartel be a meaningful element. However, we are currently trying to find IP that's meaningful, and there are a couple of projects now that I am attached as a producer. For instance, our IP person here found a book called, "Blood and Whiskey." It's about the real guy JACK DANIEL. He's a bootlegger and a womanizer. It's a period piece about how he came from nothing and built this empire. Originally, we sold it to WGN. They paid him to write the pilot script but, now that they've folded, we are out with it again. So yeah, if we are an instrumental element, we will be attached as a producer.

SV: Speaking of the IP market, it has become the way everyone is developing now. Do you feel in 10 or 15 years there will be something else that we're not thinking of that will be the new wave of developing TV shows?

GS: That's a great question. I think that IP has become so successful because no one wants to take a risk anymore. Everybody is coming from a place of fear. So, they (the network) are going to take anything that has name value, brand recognition, and, if there were people watching in the past, they are like, "Great! That can get eyeballs." Because a ton of people used to watch it twenty years ago, they are going to wheel it out, polish it up and redo it.

SV: How would you suggest a new writer get representation?

Act 4

GS: There are a million programs for diversity writers at all the networks: The ABC Fellowship Program, the Warner Brothers Writers Program, the CBS Diversity Program, the FOX Initiative.

SV: Can writers cold-call you?

GS: No. I get writers from these programs or from agents, but I think if they would call the assistants or junior agents or managers, that would be another way. We have junior managers here who are constantly telling us about writers they found and are working with. I think the way in is through assistants. Call the assistants at Imagine. Call the assistants at FOX. Any one of these millions of companies out there, they all have assistants, and say, "Hey I've got this great project. I'm a new writer. I've got this great idea. Is there anyone over there that you will think will read it? Would you read it? I've got three other production companies reading it now." You've just got to be networking in this town.

SV: What do you feel your role is in the TV Development process?

GS: Since everything now is IP, every production company in town options books and articles. So I spend a good amount of time calling them to say, "Hey, what IP are you looking for a writer on?" And then they'll say, "We just optioned..." Then they'll tell us what type of writer they're looking for, and I'll send them two or three people to consider for coming up with takes. They will usually do a kind of "bake-off" where they will have like ten people come up with ideas and then pick someone to go out with for a show.

SV: Do you work on the pitch with them to take to these production companies?

GS: Yeah, oftentimes I do, but it depends on the client. Sometimes they'll say, "Geoff, I got a take. Let me just take a meeting with the producers and I'll pitch it." And then other times they'll say like, "Here's something I'm working on. What do you think?"

And I will work with them on the idea. Sometimes they will also write spec scripts, original spec scripts because no one writes spec scripts of episodes anymore. But before they'll even write a script, I'll say, "Give me a list of loglines of scripts you're thinking of writing." And then I'll say, "I'm really gravitating towards this idea. I think you should focus on this one." They may send me a 'beat sheet,' and I'll give them notes on that. Then they send me a first draft, and I'll give them notes on that. Sometimes I've have other people here read it or they give it to their writer friends. You know, there are never too many people you can share a script with before you share it with the town. I am definitely very hands-on because we try not to bother the agents too much. They don't really have the time to do all that stuff. Managers are much more hands-on. Day-to-day, we talk to our clients all the time and really try to get the scripts in the best shape possible, and then get it out there.

SV: What is the most challenging aspect of developing with your clients?

GS: I find that it's sometimes hard to come up with a concept that's unique. Everything's been done ten ways to Sunday. It's challenging for the writer to come up with a take that is unique and jumps off the page and is going to stand out from the next guy or woman who is sending in their pilot script. So, I'm on them about finding ideas that feel fresh, super different, maybe have a hook. It has to pop off the page.

SV: What's the most rewarding?

GS: What I love as being a manager is I love calling clients when they get a job. Like when a client of mine took a six to seven year sabbatical and went on to be a teacher in a high school in Westlake and someone gave me a script he wrote. I thought it was really great. Six months later, I got him a job and he's doing it right now. He's in his second season. It's a show on Hallmark called, *Chesapeake Shores,* and he's the showrunner! When I called him to tell him that, after six months of "repping" him, he's going back to work after six years, and as a showrunner and he was going to be paid exorbitant amount of money - way more than he was making as a teacher. He was on speakerphone with his wife and they were in tears, saying, "You're an angel sent from heaven." It's so rewarding to have clients who are super-appreciative. Even today a client of mine, whom I'm not even attached as a producer, sent me this Chinese New Year two-dollar bill just because I worked so hard for them. They told me they wanted to do a show about MARIE LAVEAU, the Voodoo Queen of New Orleans in the 1800s. So I called the Wolper Organization and, before I even told them about the pitch, he's like, "We're looking for a writer for a Marie Laveau project." I told him, "We have it." So we brought it to them. They loved it and then MARK WOLPER had the idea to bring it to LEE DANIELS, and Lee loved it and attached himself as the director. Then they made a deal with FOX 21 and sold it right before the holidays to Amazon as a 'put-pilot' plus two scripts.

SV: Wow! This shows how the stars aligned for this project.

GS: Right! And tomorrow they are meeting on the spinoff of *Supernatural* because it's ending. When it works out, there's nothing better.

*****

INTERVIEW WITH MARTY BERNEMAN

Independent Talent Manager/Producer
Partner, *TheNew*Entertainment.com

*I met MARTY soon after I moved to Los Angeles from New York. We were close friends then and still are today. When I was at Spelling TV and developing the **Charmed** series for the WB network, I gave Marty the pilot script after it was completed because I was so excited about it. He shared it with a client of his, HOLLY MARIE COMBS. At the time, she was best friends with SHANNON DOHERTY, and the rest is history. Marty and I became producing partners in the mid 2000's when he was adding producer to his list of professions. The first project we put together as a team was **These Broken Stars**, which is currently being developed for Freeform, with MGM as the studio. This interview took place in January, 2018.*

Stephanie (SV): How did you get into the TV business?

Marty (MB): I have a first cousin that is a television writer, and when I was nineteen he sat me down and said, "I think you need to get into the business." I said, "No, no, no," but he really wanted me to get into this world. A year later, he was doing a pilot for ABC. He asked me to come and intern in casting and, after that, I became a PA (production assistant) on the set. I decided to try it and I worked for NAN DUTTON, a very big television casting director at that time, and that was my foray into the business.

SV: But then you segued into working at an agency?

MB: Yes. I worked at Innovative Artists Agency. Personally, I feel that a talent agency is a really important part of the business. I liken it to the central nervous system. All information that is needed in the business comes in and out of a talent agency, especially the larger ones. Without the talent agencies, nothing else would survive.

SV: What was the most challenging part of your job as a talent manager?

MB: Knowing what each client needs at a given moment in time. Each client is at a different level, and you really have to figure out what they need and anticipate what they are going to need. It was not even about getting them a job per se, it was about their specific needs and making sure you were the center of their world. The clients become an extension of your personal and professional life.

SV: What about when you switched to becoming a producer? What is the most challenging aspect?

MB: Learning the new players. As a talent manager, I was talking to the heads of casting at each studio. As a producer, I needed to find out and get to know the development executives. These were new sets of individuals that I didn't know. If I didn't know who the player was, I would call the casting person at the studio or network that I worked with and ask them to set up a meeting for me. They would always come through because I had a relation-ship with these leaders of the industry for the past twenty years.

SV: What is your advice for writers just starting out?

MB: Get into a writing group, writing workshop. Act as if you are part of the business. There are all these different things that you can do. You need to immerse yourself into the business in order to find out who the players are, who you need to talk to, who is that connection to x, y and z. It's really about who you know. Also, now that we have the internet, you can write a web-series. Go and do something small and get it self-produced. You can't sit on your ass! You have to go out there and do. No one is coming to you. You got to go to them.

Act 4

SV: What advice do you have for non-writing producers wanting to produce TV shows?

MB: It's all about material, material, material. Find yourself a hot book or an IP. Find that source, whether it's a great script, article, book, foreign television show, comic book series, who knows... that's one thing. Then align yourself with someone, a writer, another producer, an actor. Then figure out what is your brand. I think that's the thing. Know who you are and what you are good at selling!

SV: Do you have a strategy for selling a TV show?

MB: Cover your bases. Are you represented? Do you have a manager or an agent? Next, where does your material fit? If it's an HBO series, then you have to figure out how to connect to the HBO network. Be sure not to take your show to the wrong place. For instance, if you were selling *The Good Wife*, you wouldn't have tried to sell that to HBO. Know your audience. That's the key.

SV: What was the first TV show where you were part of the TV Development process?

MB: When I was a manager, I was very involved with the first-ever Hulu series called, *Battleground*. They wanted my client for the lead. It was interesting to watch that process, because at the time they didn't have a lot of money and almost everyone didn't understand streaming television. I read the script and, actually in this case, we got the full-season of episodes to read - all 10 episodes. The fact that we got to read the whole season and see where it goes was an anomaly. I read them and thought there is no way my client is not doing this. I remember having a call with his agent where I said, "I really think he needs to do this," and she said, "Over my dead body." I told her that this is the future. He ultimately did do it and now he works all the time. Actually, I just heard they are putting the cast back together to do a second season now - seven years later.

SV: What do you feel will be different about TV in the next five years, ten years?

MB: I can already see that, over the last year (2017), CBS has created an all-access app that you can use on all your devices. I think they are the first broadcast network to be producing content for their own app. No other network is doing this yet. I think they are being very smart about it because I don't think broadcast television will be very strong in the next five years. I think it's going to be all about our devices, and network television, in the traditional sense, is going to die. If you look at CDs, DVDs, Blockbusters, they don't exist anymore. I think the next thing to go is cable. I believe we will all have apps for the different networks and studios, and you're going to be able to pick and choose whatever you want. There is not going to be a need for a television set per se.

*****

ADVICE FROM TOP NETWORK EXECUTIVES

I interviewed the TOP EXECUTIVES at A PREMIUM AND A BROADCAST NETWORK in August, 2018. Unfortunately their networks' prohibited me from publishing them, so I paraphrased the information from the interview to share with you.

THE TV DEVELOPMENT PROCESS

One of the development executives felt that most TV shows are developed the "TV way." Meaning, there's a lot of material out there and someone will call and tell the network executives about it. Or they are developed the "movie way," which is there's a lot of material out there and the network executives have to find it and go after it themselves. Also, networks are presented with a tremendous amount of scripts. In the development process the truth is, it's inevitable there are great scripts that don't get made and lesser scripts that do.

One big consideration for the networks is time constraints. They have only so much time to develop a project with someone (aka the writer). There comes a point when a project may be taking too long or a point where there is just not enough time to work on that project. Most networks have a cycle for developing shows. It's about six months long, and then they decide if they are going forward with it or not. However, there are a few networks out there today that will develop a show for years. This is more like feature development.

They talked about how network executives are notorious for giving writers plenty of notes, but they expressed that the key is to be careful when they express themselves. They know many writers can be sensitive about their material and even though writers want to hear what the networks have to say, they'd really prefer to be complimented. So a network executive must walk a fine line. They can't insult the writer, yet they need to convey everything that has to be changed or modified. They agree it's important for networks to understand what the writer is trying to accomplish in each idea put forth.

One executive talked about how SYDNEY POLLACK is a legend in this business because he was one of the first people to be Socratic about how he gave notes, meaning he would ask many questions. His questions were encouraging while pointing out what was wrong with the script. In doing so he was able to elicit understandable and workable solutions.

Therefore, during the script development phase, a network executive might ask the writer, "What are you trying to do in that scene?" "What do you want me to understand about this part?" "What can we do to make this better?" This way the writer won't feel too harshly criticized. Another important skill for executives to have is to be a good listener. They have to tell writers what they think and make sure they are getting their points across, yet they also must listen carefully to what writers are trying to say. Only then can they work effectively together.

There is general consensus in today's marketplace that writers and/or producers are at a disadvantage if they don't have a book or an IP. Network executives believe the reason people get the rights to books is because it is a great springboard to be able to start with something that already exists. There are hundreds and hundreds of words on the subject already, so that is a preference for the writer/producer and the networks. Also, movie stars will eagerly sign on for eight hours of a book adaptation.

THE PROCESS FOR SHOWS GETTING 'GREEN LIT'

At most networks, developing a TV show is an arduous process. There's testing and company-wide meetings with all different divisions and departments. Yet there are a few networks that have a very small group deciding on everything that gets made. They don't test, or ask anyone else. It's up to a small group of executives.

PITCHING ADVICE

Make it *interesting*! Every place will want to know your idea and storyline in about two to three minutes. It's important for writers to explain what their show is about in a simple way while getting others curious and excited about what comes next, who the characters are, and what they are going to do in series (for the episodes).

The network executives advised that it is important to do research and learn the interests, focuses and culture of the networks to which you are trying to sell. This can make or break selling your show. Your producers and agents may also be able to give you insight on some of the nuances.

It is also important to have a fresh perspective. There are over 500 scripted shows on the air, so obviously not everything you pitch will be right for a particular network. Networks end up passing on most prospective shows. These days, you really do need to stand out from the pack.

THE BUYERS HAVE DIFFERENT FOCUSES AT BROADCAST VS. BASIC CABLE

The buyers at broadcast networks purchase a greater number of TV shows/series than the buyers at cable networks. They have more resources and can get a project if they really want it. The big difference is they look for programming that has broad appeal. When "big names" come to broadcast networks, they have to move quickly because of there is a lot of competition.

Cable networks are more boutique operations. They generally cater to a more niche audiences. They are very focused on how much can be spent and how to beat the competition. Also, they are much more limited as to the offers they can make.

ADVICE FOR YOUNG WRITERS AND DEVELOPMENT EXECUTIVES

For writers, start with writing as much as you can. You need to develop a body of work so you can figure out who you are as a writer. In this way, you will develop your own writing style and learn your own voice. You should write something that is close to your own experiences. In other words, write what you know.

A good way to start out as a development executive begins with a stint at a talent agency. Then you can work for a production company, studio, network, or all of the above. Another option is to enroll in this author's course at UCLA, "TV Development: From Idea to Small Screen." (*This was unsolicited*)

THE MEASURE OF A SUCCESSFUL SHOW IN TODAY'S MARKET

Ratings still matter and awards do help. The hardest thing to quantify that means the most today is the 'cultural impact' a show can have. Network executives agree that if someone can create a show that impacts our culture in some way, it makes it more appealing. This can be an idea that impacts us socially, has people talking about it, helps people see a different point of view, influences other media, etc.

Whether you're in broadcast, cable or streaming, the buyers believe that shows that culturally influence us in some way will probably have the greatest impact on us.

*****

ADVICE FROM TOP LITERARY AGENTS

I interviewed LITERARY AGENTS FROM TOP TALENT AGENCIES in January and February, 2018. Unfortunately the agencies prohibited me from publishing them, so I paraphrased the information from the interview to share with you.

THE DIFFERENCES BETWEEN A MANAGER AND AN AGENT

Traditionally, agents are tasked with getting people jobs and managers spend their time developing material. Agents work in volume, and managers get into the nitty-gritty with fewer people. They felt it is a personal preference. However, many agents become managers, and many managers become agents.

They felt that managers are in a better position today than they were 15 years ago. They have become more essential to the business as evidenced by the fact that they are a part of the majority of TV shows on the air. Agents, on the other hand, have even more options. They get to represent a lot more material, projects, volume, etc. They also tend to work for a larger companies.

THE AGENT'S ROLE IN THE TV DEVELOPMENT PROCESS

Agents felt that it was key for them to know the marketplace, i.e., what different buyers are looking for, and anything else that might help their client's idea have a better chance of selling to a particular outlet.

Most important, agents should be an advocates for their clients' ideas. Agents represent the storytellers who might come to them and say, "I want to do this." Conversely, agents can bring ideas to their clients. Maybe an agent sees a great piece of material and realizes she or he knows of a writer who might be perfect for the project. Whether it's a book, an article, or an old television show idea that could be redone, their main role is to be an advocate. Agents try to get as much IP product as possible and bring it to their clients.

Also, they like to put their clients together. If an actor comes to an agent with an idea, the agent will try to find the right client to attach to the project. Sometimes they do it to help nurture a project along.

One factor agents consider is how the client enters the process. If the client has a spec script that they've written, the agent will read the script, evaluate it, and most likely help them. They would probably give mostly macro notes because agents who get into the very small details with notes would be spending too much time on development. Agents said it was more of the manager's job. Agents don't have time for that the way a manager or a producer might. There are also many different uses for a script. Agents can try to sell it, use it as a writing sample for development, or even for staffing purposes.

NON-WRITING PRODUCERS WHO WANT TO PRODUCE TV SHOWS

Across the board, agents agreed it is imperative to have the best IP, or the best material, that you can get your hands on. Let's say, for example, you are the person who has the rights to *Big, Little Lies*. You would become a very important person in the mix. The person who had the rights to *Game of Thrones* never produced a TV show before! The process is arduous, but if you have the right IP you become indispensable.

Perhaps you have a relationship with talent? Maybe you optioned a script? The person who optioned *True Detective*, as well as *Ozark*, was from outside the business. Therefore, if you are the person who identifies (and gets the rights to) a great piece of material, that would surely work in your favor.

HOW AGENTS PREPARE THEIR CLIENTS TO PITCH IN THE MARKETPLACE

If a client walks in with an idea, the agent will listen and try to determine if the show has a specific point of view because, they emphasized how important it is for a show to have one. If it's just a kernel of an idea, the agent may ask the writer to expand upon it so that it can last for many hours on television. This is different than a movie, which is two hours in and out.

The agents say that, in TV, no one is particularly interested in the just the pilot. Pilots alone don't sell TV shows. TV buyers want to know that the show has a long, extended narrative. The agent and writer will determine that beforehand. Then they will decide if it is commercial enough and if there's a buyer for it. The good news is that there are so many buyers in the marketplace today there might be a home for just about anything.

Another type of pitch is when you are selling a show that originates from a book or an IP. The agent will put the book, or IP together with the right writer, or non-writing producer, and then figure out where to market it.

HOW A NEW WRITER CAN GET REPRESENTATION

Having a great piece of material is the most important factor. Writers should be writing all the time, not only to improve their craft, but also to develop future material.

It is important to build a strong network of friends and relationships. You could start out by working at a studio or on a production. If you want to be a TV writer, try to work for people making television shows. They are going to become advocates for you from within. Work the head writer on a show and get him or her to read your script. They are more likely to read your script before they read someone else's.

Act 4

Another skill a writer should have is being "good in a room." You should be enthusiastic and well-versed. Remember that the people you will meet with have probably seen all the TV shows and movies that are related to your work in any way.

PITCHING A TV SHOW

It has to be the best pitch possible, which includes a clear idea of the world you are painting and the characters you are creating.

The agents said you really don't have to pitch the story as much as the total concept. (This does depends on the kind of show you are doing, i.e., franchise vs. serialized.) You want to set up the world and then the characters. The networks should be able to see that there's a show there. For example, if you were pitching *The Sopranos* and described it as, "a mafia boss in therapy," the networks could (and did) imagine many potential conflicts and stories that could come out of this set-up, and what a rich world it could develop into. Your story should be able to last multiple seasons. That's what you want to convey in a pitch.

SHOULD YOU ATTACH A STUDIO BEFORE GOING TO THE NETWORKS?

That depends on your idea and what networks you are targeting. Today there is a lot of "vertical integration" in the industry. This means that many studios and networks are subdivisions of the same company. Professionals say that projects coming in from related companies are going to have a better chance of being successfully produced. Therefore, if you believe your project is perfect for a particular cable company or network, consider bringing it to that sister studio first.

Also, it is critical, in both the comedy and drama worlds, to be working with people who are experienced and have relationships everywhere. You need someone that the networks would buy from. But the most important person will always be the writer and/or the showrunner. Furthermore, having a big producer, director, or talent in your corner would, of course, be very helpful.

THOUGHTS ABOUT SPEC SCRIPTS

The professionals felt that, in today's marketplace, it is advantageous to have spec scripts because that is what the networks are looking for. Although plays and screenplays (movie scripts) are also welcome, the agents said that original TV material/TV pilots are the key.

They said there are certain types of writers who would benefit by developing spec scripts. Let's say a writer has a strong vision for a TV show, but has trouble articulating it in a pitch. Perhaps a writer doesn't want his or her original concept going through too many hands where it might be changed. They would be well-advised to write spec scripts.

Writing a spec gives the writer total control until selling it to a network. If it is exceptional, the networks will buy it. An important downside is that the writer does *not* get paid while writing it.

Agents wanted to advise writers to have more than one sample of their work. But, above all, their main advice was - never stop writing! Keep creating.

FOR WRITERS/CREATORS LOOKING TO SELL A TV SHOW

Do your homework. Learn from people who are doing it by watching all the shows that are out there. Educate yourself on why they work as TV shows. Be open to any kind of criticism and any information you get to make your show better. When you go out to sell, be prepared for every question you are going to be asked. If someone is interested in buying your show, you're going to get a lot of them. Have the answers. There are usually no wrong answers, but you should have your opinion and be open to modifications during the TV Development process. If it's going to make the difference of someone buying your show or not, don't be uncompromising with your material. It is their network so they should have some input.

Act 4

THE REALITY WHEN SELLING SHOWS

When you go out with a project, the answer you will hear most often is "No." You will get very few yeses, and hopefully take the no's in stride. You must stay focused on your goal and be resilient. From the pitch stage to getting a series order, this is part of the process.

MISCONCEPTIONS ABOUT TV DEVELOPMENT

People who aren't in the business may think it's all about a great idea. The truth is that much of it is dictated by who is going to be executing the show. If you watch a great television show and look at the credits you'll see that there are master storytellers, master filmmakers and master actors… along with that great idea.

Also, writers and producers have to determine if an idea should become a TV show or a movie. There are a lot of great ideas that just aren't suited for TV. People often misjudge what a great TV show idea is. For example, a great televised event is not necessarily considered a great TV show. A great TV show is one that becomes a series and lives over a long period of time.

INDEPENDENTLY PRODUCING AND SELLING YOUR OWN TV SHOW

The perception from agents is that it is very risky. Most people who attempt to independently produce their own show lose money. The upside of independently producing TV shows is that you (or whomever financed it) will own the show, be able to develop it creatively without network input or interference and sell it (domestically and internationally). This will give you the most profit. Keep in mind that producing a television show is extremely expensive. It is not easy for most of us to find someone who is willing to put up that kind of money, has faith that the show will work internationally, and be able to put all the pieces together. However, here are some of the reputable/successful independent financiers in television today: MRC, Gaumont Television, and Sonar Entertainment.

Act 4

THE FUTURE OF THE TV DEVELOPMENT PROCESS

Twenty years ago the TV Development process was focused on a pitch. Nowadays you still need the pitch, but you can write a spec script and/or make a sizzle reel to get your project out there - and you can make a sizzle reel for very little money! This will hopefully lead to getting a series order more quickly.

The agents believe the future of the process probably won't be much different than it is today. But judging from how fast technology is advancing, you will probably have even more ways to get your idea out there.

THOUGHTS ON SUCCESS IN TODAY'S LANDSCAPE

For a show to be successful, the agents believe that it's not about critical acclaim or even ratings. They agree that it's all about profitability. If your show is making money, it will have a much better chance of staying on the air.

*****

ACT FIVE

Final Thoughts

BEYOND THE PILOT

In order to have a successful TV series, it is necessary to show that your story goes on far beyond the pilot. I cannot stress this enough. This is why the development of your series before you sell it will be a big part of the reason for its success or failure.

Before trying to sell your series, going through the development process and working out the bible will give you a big leg up for success. Also, being open and flexible to the process is key. (*See Act 2, "What is a Bible for a TV Series"*)

Today, there are so many different shows on the air that the audience has become fractured. This is one of the many reason shows are dropped after the first few episodes or first season.

In this regard, the following are excerpts from, "Among Broadcast Networks," at Screenrant.com.

Act 5

"Looking back on the programming decisions made by the networks from 2009-2012, you may be surprised to find out that, on average, 65% of new network television series will be canceled within their first season. Completely acknowledging the fact that television, like all entertainment, is a largely subjective medium, the numbers do not actually represent the quality of the television series on the air. Even though more than half of the new shows will be canceled, that doesn't mean that more than half aren't of quality - or worth watching. Nor does it represent the demographic of the networks' audience or the impact that demographics have on ad revenue.

Instead, these numbers represent, at their core, a network's ability to not only appropriately select programming for its audience (including potential), but to also schedule in such a way to allow for a series' success. As many fans of cult television shows know, perhaps more than anyone, even a quality series can fail solely because of a given time-slot. Providing much more than simply the amount of new series that will be canceled, the numbers also reveal that out of all the broadcast networks, new television series on ABC have the highest chance of receiving a second season - with an average 39% chance of renewal. Trailing not far behind, Fox and CBS have 38% and 36%, respectively.

This is an interesting placement for Fox, considering they only have to schedule programming from 8pm-10pm, instead of 8pm-11pm like most networks. Even with a portion of the pick-ups comparable to other networks, ABC still managed to come out on top with these statistics, though Fox is currently considered the #1 broadcast network."

If you are fortunate enough to get through to the third season, networks will usually keep the show going for at least another couple of seasons. The idea or chance of getting past five to seven seasons is a long life of a first-run show in today's landscape. It seems that longer running shows are a thing of the past (e.g., *Law and Order, CSI, Simpsons, SNL*), but not impossible.

TELEVISION VIEWERSHIP

The following was reported by Nielsen Media Research, television's leading premier rating service.

"Today's (2017) media landscape is ever changing, but it's also growing. Adults in the U.S. are spending an additional half hour more a day compared to last year connected to media across platforms—digital, audio and television—which are the three platforms of content distribution and discovery for the average consumer. And these devices have become a constant companion to over 200 million consumers in the U.S. and this personalized entertainment is always at their fingertips.

As of June 2017, 58.7% (or 69.5 million) of TV Households own at least one internet-enabled device that is capable of streaming content to the television set.   This includes an enabled multimedia device, an enabled smart TV and an enabled video game console. "

According to the Statistic Brain Research Institute in 2017:

99% of households have a television with 2.24 TVs per household.

67% of Americans watch TV while eating dinner.

47% say they watch too much TV.

The amount of years the average person will have spent watching TV over their lifetime: 9

The average amount of time a youth spends in school per year: 900 hours

The average amount of time a youth spends watching TV per year: 1200 hours

Act 5

According to the Bureau of Labor Statistics Leisure Activities in 2017 were as follows;

"On an average day, nearly everyone age 15 and over (96 percent) engaged in some sort of leisure activity, such as watching TV, socializing, or exercising. Men spent 33 minutes per day more in these activities than did women (5.5 hours, compared with 5.0 hours).

Watching TV was the leisure activity that occupied the most time (2.8 hours per day), accounting for just over half of all leisure time, on average. The amount of time people spent watching TV varied by age. Those ages 15 to 44 spent the least amount of time watching TV, averaging around 2.0 hours per day, and those ages 65 and over spent the most time watching TV, averaging over 4.0 hours per day." (*See table p.160*)

HOUSEHOLD OWNERSHIP OF ENABLED DEVICES (ONE, TWO OR THREE)

Of the 58.7% of TV Households that have an enabled device...

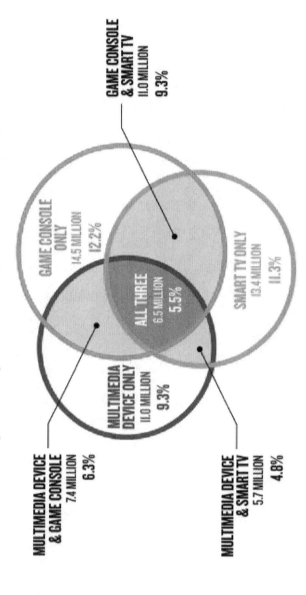

GAME CONSOLE & SMART TV
11.0 MILLION
9.3%

GAME CONSOLE ONLY
14.5 MILLION
12.2%

SMART TV ONLY
13.4 MILLION
11.3%

ALL THREE
6.5 MILLION
5.5%

MULTIMEDIA DEVICE ONLY
11.0 MILLION
9.3%

MULTIMEDIA DEVICE & GAME CONSOLE
7.4 MILLION
6.3%

MULTIMEDIA DEVICE & SMART TV
5.7 MILLION
4.8%

WHAT SOME ACTORS HAVE SAID ABOUT WORKING IN TV:

"I feel like some of the best talent is on TV right now, with the writing, acting and great directors. I've also been looking for the consistency of work that TV provides for you. And, I always thought it would be really interesting to live with a character for months, if not years." CHRISTINA RICCI (*Brainyquote.com*)

"I wanted to be involved in TV and film in some capacity, so a compromise, because acting seemed unrealistic, and so risky, was to get into the production side. And it was a really fortunate, smart move looking back on it, because it gave me perspective on another side of the business." WENTWORTH MILLER (*Brainyquote.com*)

"When you're doing a TV show, it's not like you just shoot for six weeks and you're in an editing room with all of your footage. It's like a guitar or a car, you have to fine tune things. You stop doing what's not working, you work on what is working and you add things that do work." CHRIS PRATT (*Brainyquote.com*)

"I don't have real big aspirations to be a movie star. I would love to be on a long-running hit TV show. You end up playing a defining role." JENNA FISCHER (*Brainyquote.com*)

TAKE NOTE

Most TV shows don't make it to the small screen. According to Wikipedia.com, in 2018 it categorized 45 pages of "Unaired Produced Pilots." Each year, millions of dollars are spent on pilots that don't get picked up to series. But every show that does get on TV, on all the networks, cable and streaming platforms, shows you that you can beat the odds and get a show on the air!

Another thing to consider is that your TV show may change as time goes by due to many influences beyond your control, such as budget constraints, actors, directors, life, and timing. But the hope is that your show/pilot gets better and better even through delays and detours.

FINAL TAKES

YOU HAVE NOW COMPLETED A COURSE IN TV DEVELOPMENT!

CONGRATULATIONS!

You have acquired the tools you need to sell your ideas because you have studied the processes and heard from the experts.

Also, you have a pre-requisite for becoming a TV Development executive, TV writer or TV producer. I hope you feel you have a good understanding and a greater appreciation of what it takes to develop and sell a TV show.

WHAT DO YOU DO NOW?

If you are interested in becoming a:

■ **Development/Current Executive** at a network, streaming service or a studio:

- Get in the door at one of the big companies and start as an assistant.

- Read, learn, network!

■ **Agent or Manager:**

- Sign up for a company's training program.

- Network and read!

■ **Writer:**

- Keep writing.

- Submit online.

- Get in a writing program.

■ **Producer:**

- Keep working.

- Find great material.

■ **Director:**

- Keep directing. Work on your craft.

- Get a job working for a director.

■ **Most Important For All:**

- NEVER GIVE UP!

NOW, GO MAKE YOUR TV SHOW!

When you do get your show in production, you will have a chance to hire a director (unless one is already attached), a staff of writers (it's critical to get the best), a cast, and all the below-the-line producers and production crew who will figure out everything necessary to transform what is on the page to the small screen. Seeing your hard work grow from a mere idea and come to life on the screen is no less than wonderful.

SUCCESS

In my experience, when a show gets on the air and continues for several seasons, it is exhilarating! It's a great experience for you, the audience, the networks, the studios, and everyone involved.

My years in television production have been very rewarding to me; professionally, personally, and financially. On top of that, I truly enjoyed working on every show I have been a part of. That is why I am so enthusiastic about this business.

GLOSSARY
Terms used in the TV industry

ACQUIRED CONTENT: TV shows that previously aired on one network are then purchased by another network to broadcast.

ACT BREAKS: Places where a TV show is divided up to allow for commercials.

AGENCY PACKAGE: Talent agencies represent key people or companies attached to a show. They receive a fee from the production for every episode.

ATTACHMENTS: Key people and companies to add to your project when developing it.

BEAT SHEET: A bullet-point outline of a pilot or concept for a TV series.

BELOW THE LINE: Crew members that work on the production of a TV or film.

BIBLE: A document that details the extended plan for the series. It would include all of the character descriptions, themes, tone, world and have episode ideas and/or arcs for the characters.

BRAND: How a network is in the marketplace as evidenced by their choice of programming, target audience, marketing focus, development objectives, etc.

BREAK THE STORY: A term used by writers on a show when they are fleshing out the plot and character arcs for a series.

BUYERS LIST: A list of all the networks, including streaming outlets. A buyer is any network who will pay for content to air.

COLD CALL: A term used when you don't know executives personally, but call to see if you can get a meeting for your project.

COMPETITIVE DEVELOPMENT REPORT: A list of what projects the networks are actively buying for development.

COVERAGE: A report that an agent, manager, producer or executive asks a reader to put together on a script or book.

DEFICIT FINANCE: The amount of money it costs a studio to produce an episode above the network's license fee.

FIRST RUN: The first airing of a show on a network.

FLYER: When a network will take a risk with a particular project.

GREEN-LIGHT: When a project is moving into the production phase.

HIP-POCKETING CLIENTS: When an agent or manager does not formally represent someone, but they are working with them on the side.

INDIE TV: When you receive independent financing to produce a pilot and/or a season(s) of a show.

INTELLECTUAL PROPERTY (IP): Published or produced works. This would include articles, books, comic books, graphic novels, someone's life rights (past or present), short stories, poems, blogs, past TV shows, foreign TV shows and movies.

LICENSE FEE: A fee that networks pay studios, per episode, for the rights to air their shows.

LOGLINE: One or two sentences describing what the TV series or movie is about.

NOTES: These are thoughts that are given to writers about their material.

OPTION AGREEMENT: A contract where the person proposing for the agreement/producer pays the rights upfront, and everything is negotiated before the producer can attempt to sell it.

PACKAGE: All the people and organizations affiliated in any way to a project.

PAGE NOTES: Small thoughts on a specific page of a script.

PITCH: A verbal presentation of a project from the writers and producers to a studio or network.

PITCH DOCUMENT: A blueprint for the pitch. Producers and writers use this as a tool for preparing the pitch before going out to the networks.

POINTS: A legal term used in contracts regarding the sharing of profits on a project.

PRIME TIME: Term used to describe when adults, ages 18-49, the most coveted demographic, watch television. It's TV viewing after dinner and before bedtime, or from 8:00-10:00 p.m.

PROCEDURALS: Dramas (could be comedies as well) that have stand-alone episodes. They do not need to be watched in order. Sometimes called franchises.

PUT-PILOT: Term used when an idea is sold and the network makes a commitment to shoot the pilot before a script is written.

READERS: People who are paid to read a script or book and write a report on it, similar to a book report. They can be a professional reader for hire, an assistant or a lower level executive.

Glossary

REBOOT: An updated version of an old TV show or movie.

REVERSE ENGINEER: A strategy used to manipulate an idea to better accommodate a particular market.

SERIALIZED: A series that has episodes which are connected and must be watched in order.

SHOPPING AGREEMENT: A contract where there is no upfront cost for the person proposing the agreement (the producer). This gives the producer the right to try to sell the project for a specified amount of time.

SHOWRUNNER: The writing executive producer on a TV series. They are responsible for everything from the writing to the production of the show.

SISTER STUDIO: A production company that is attached to a network.

SIZZLE REEL: A video presentation, or proof of concept, for the pitch of a project.

SPEC SCRIPT: A pilot script written before being commissioned or paid. This is a sample of a writer's writing skills and voice.

STAFF WRITER: The entry-level position for a writer on a TV series.

STANDARDS AND PRACTICES: Rules networks must adhere to that control the content of their shows.

STORY AREA: The first document presented after a script is commissioned by a network. It consists of the general story of the pilot episode.

TEASER: The opening scene of a TV show.

Glossary

TREATMENT: This is usually the first document a writer presents that gives details about his or her idea.

TV TALENT: The department in talent agencies that represent actors (as opposed to the literary departments which represent writers and directors).

TV DEVELOPMENT: The department in networks, studios and production companies that work with writers on ideas and strategies for TV shows.

WORLD: Where a TV show takes place, i.e., setting, location, time period, etc.

WRITERS LIST: A list of potential writers that development executives and producers put together for specific projects.

SPECIAL THANKS

I would like to thank Bobbi Michaels, Yvette Lowenthal-Mulderry, Jill Karnick-Grill, Jill Cote, Stephanie Stein, Deb Weisberg, Karen Horwitz, Nicole and Larry Seymour, Eric Balfour and Marty Berneman for all their love and support over the years, it means the world to me.

ABOUT THE AUTHOR

Stephanie Varella is a partner in the independent production company, *TheNew*Entertainment.com; the creator and instructor of "TV Development: From Idea to Small Screen," a class in the Entertainment Studies department at UCLA; and a professional TV expert/consultant/owner of TVDevelopmentCoach.com.

As Vice President of Series Development and Production at Jerry Bruckheimer TV and Development Executive at Spelling Entertainment, she developed and worked on such hit TV shows as *CSI, CSI: NY, CSI: MIAMI, Without a Trace, Cold Case, Amazing Race, Charmed, 7th Heaven, Any Day Now* and *The New Love Boat*. Stephanie is in development, or has developed shows, with *all* the major studios and broadcast/cable networks and is currently selling to the newer streaming platforms. One of her unscripted shows is in development with Collins Ave. and one of her scripted shows is in development with MGM based on a *NY Times Best Selling* Book Series.

Made in the USA
San Bernardino, CA
20 June 2020